HEROS DE L'ÂGE D'OR À DESSINER!

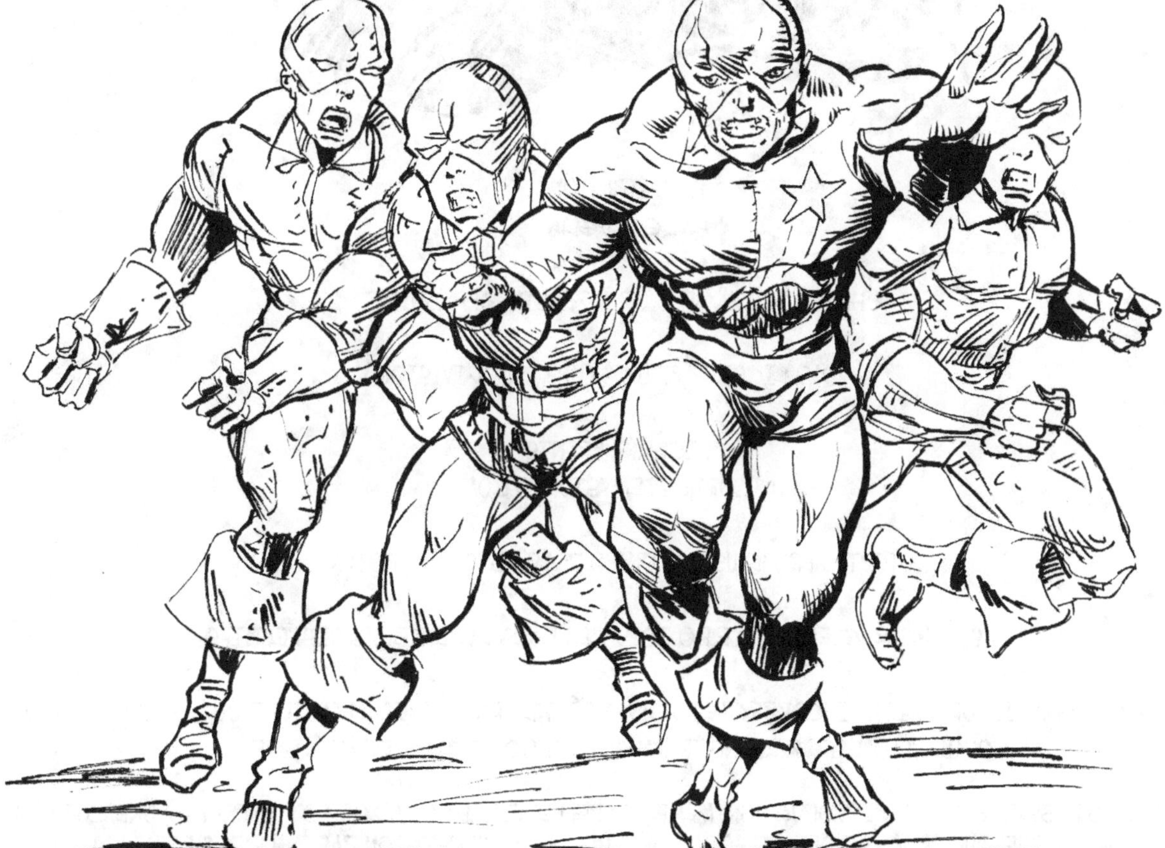

GUIDE

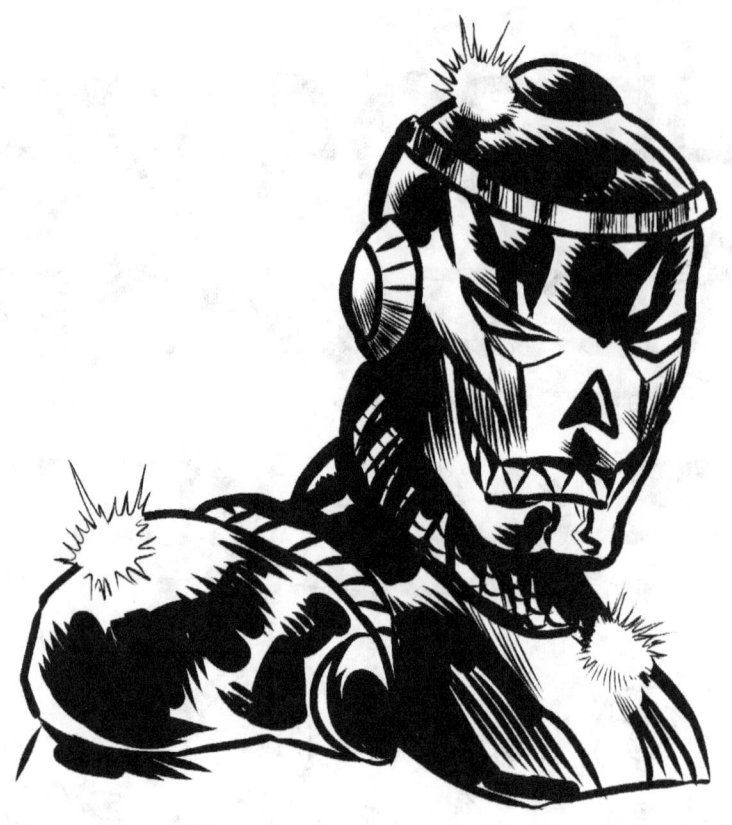

ILLUSTRATIONS:
A. G. CEGLIA

HEROS DE L'ÂGE D'OR À DESSINER! - GUIDE

© 2019 LICORNE PRINTS (UNE BMS DIVISION).

LICORNE PRINTS
LICORNE@BEMYSTUDIO.COM

TOUTES LES ILLUSTRATIONS © 2019 LICORNE PRINTS

TOUS LES CARACTÈRES TM ET © 2019 DE LEURS DÉTENTEURS RESPECTIFS

TOUTE OMMISSION OU INFORMATIONS INCORRECTES DOIVENT ÊTRE TRANSMISES À L'AUTEUR OU L'ÉDITEUR DE SORTE QU'IL PEUT ÊTRE RECTIFIÉE DANS L'ÉDITION FUTURE DE CE LIVRE.

TOUS DROITS RÉSERVÉS. TOUTE REPRODUCTION, MÊME PARTIELLE, DE CET OUVRAGE EST INTERDITE. UNE COPIE OU REPRODUCTION PAR QUELQUE PROCEED QUE CE SOIT CONSTITUE UNE CONTREFAÇON PASSABLE DES PEINES PRÉVUES PAR LE LOI INTERNATIONALE SUR LA PROTECTION DES DROITS D'AUTEUR.

IMPRIMÉ PAR CREATESPACE, UNE SOCIÉTÉ AMAZON.COM
DISPONIBLE SUR AMAZON.COM, CREATESPACE.COM, ET D'AUTRES POINTS DE VENTE.

LISTE DES CARACTÈRES

ALIAS THE DRAGON
(HARRY "A" CHESLER, SKYROCKET COMICS –ONE SHOT, 1944)

ATOMIC THUNDERBOLT
(REGOR COMPANY, ATOMIC THUNDERBOLT #1, FEB. 1946)

BARRY KUDA & ALGIE
(HARRY "A" CHESLER, YANKEE COMICS #2, NOV. 1941)

BLACK DWARF
(HARRY "A" CHESLER, SPOTLIGHT COMICS #1, NOV. 1944)

BLACK SATAN
(HARRY "A" CHESLER, YANKEE COMICS #1, SEPT. 1941)

BLACK TERROR
(BETTER/NEDOR/STANDARD, EXCITING COMICS #9, MAY 1941)

CAPTAIN BATTLE & KANE
(HARRY "A" CHESLER, CAPTAIN BATTLE COMICS #3, WINTER 1942)

CAPTAIN GLORY
(HARRY "A" CHESLER, PUNCH COMICS #1, DEC. 1941)

DR. FROST
(PRIZE, PRIZE COMICS #7, DEC. 1940)

DR. VAMPIRE
(HARRY "A" CHESLER, SKYROCKET COMICS #1, 1944)

DYNAMIC BOY, DYNAMIC MAN'S SIDEKICK
(HARRY "A" CHESLER, DYNAMIC COMICS #11, SEPT. 1944)

DYNAMIC MAN
(HARRY "A" CHESLER, DYNAMIC COMICS #1, OCT. 1941)

ECHO
(HARRY "A" CHESLER, YANKEE COMICS #1, SEPT. 1941)

ENCHANTED DAGGER
(HARRY "A" CHESLER, YANKEE COMICS #1, SEPT. 1941)

FIGHTING YANK
(BETTER/NEDOR/STANDARD, STARTLING COMICS #10, SEPT. 1941)

FIREBRAND
(HARRY "A" CHESLER, YANKEE COMICS #1, SEPT. 1941)

FOUR COMRADES
(BETTER/NEDOR/STANDARD, STARTLING COMICS #16, AUG. 1942)

GREEN KNIGHT & LANCE
(HARRY "A" CHESLER, DYNAMIC COMICS #2, DEC. 1941)

HALE THE MAGICIAN
(HARRY "A" CHESLER, DYNAMIC COMICS #1, SEPT. 1941)

JOHNNY REBEL
(HARRY "A" CHESLER, YANKEE COMICS #2, NOV. 1941)

JUDY OF THE JUNGLE
(BETTER/NEDOR/STANDARD, EXCITING COMICS #55, MAY 1947)

KAZA
(AJAX-FARRELL, FANTASTIC FEARS #8, JUL.-AUG. 1954)

KITTY KELLY
(HARRY "A" CHESLER, PUNCH COMICS #1, DEC. 1941)

LADY SATAN
(HARRY "A" CHESLER, DYNAMIC COMICS #2, DEC. 1941)

MASTER KEY
(HARRY "A" CHESLER, SCOOP COMICS #1, NOV. 1941)

MEKANO
(BETTER/NEDOR/STANDARD, WONDER COMICS #1, MAY 1944)

MR. E
(HARRY "A" CHESLER, PUNCH COMICS #1, DEC. 1941)

MISS MASQUE
(BETTER/NEDOR/STANDARD, EXCITING COMICS #51, SEPT. 1946)

MOTHER HUBBARD
(HARRY "A" CHESLER, SCOOP COMICS #1, NOV. 1941)

PHANTOM DETECTIVE
(BETTER/NEDOR/STANDARD, THRILLING COMICS #53, APR. 1946)

QUEEN MERMA, BARRY KUDA'S GIRLFRIEND
(HARRY "A" CHESLER, YANKEE COMICS #2, NOV. 1941)

ROCKET BOY
(HARRY "A" CHESLER, SCOOP COMICS #2, JAN. 1942)

ROCKETMAN & ROCKETGIRL
(HARRY "A" CHESLER, SCOOP COMICS #1, NOV. 1941)

SPIDER WOMAN
(HARRY "A" CHESLER, MAJOR VICTORY COMICS #1, 1944)

VEILED AVENGER
(HARRY "A" CHESLER, SPOTLIGHT COMICS #1, NOV. 1944)

YANKEE DOODLE JONES & DANDY
(HARRY "A" CHESLER, YANKEE COMICS #1, SEPT. 1941)

YANKEE BOY
(HARRY "A" CHESLER, YANKEE COMICS #2, NOV. 1941)

YANKEE GIRL
(HARRY "A" CHESLER, DYNAMIC COMICS #23, 1947)

HÉROS D'ENCRAGE!

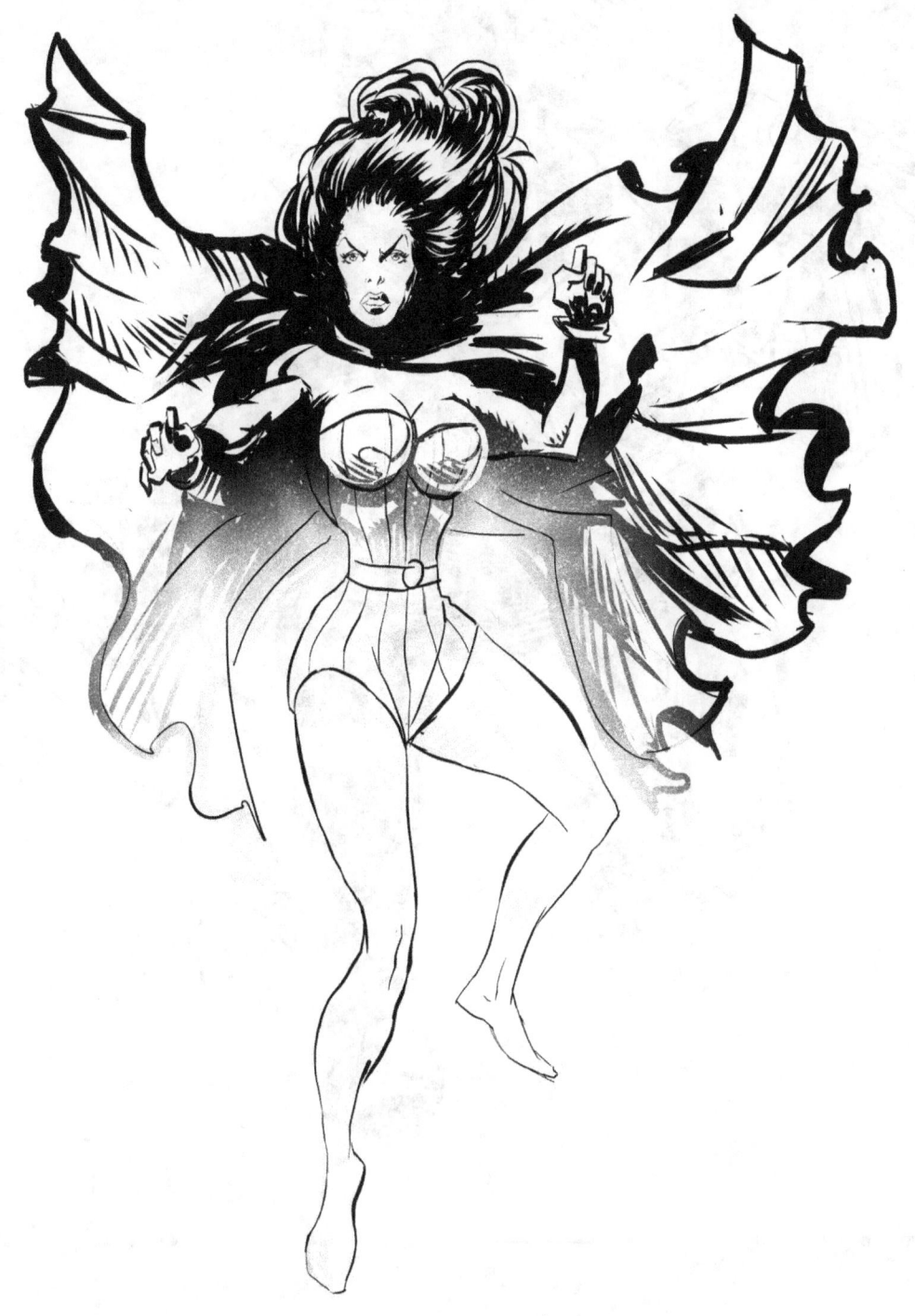

ENCRES CARACTÈRE

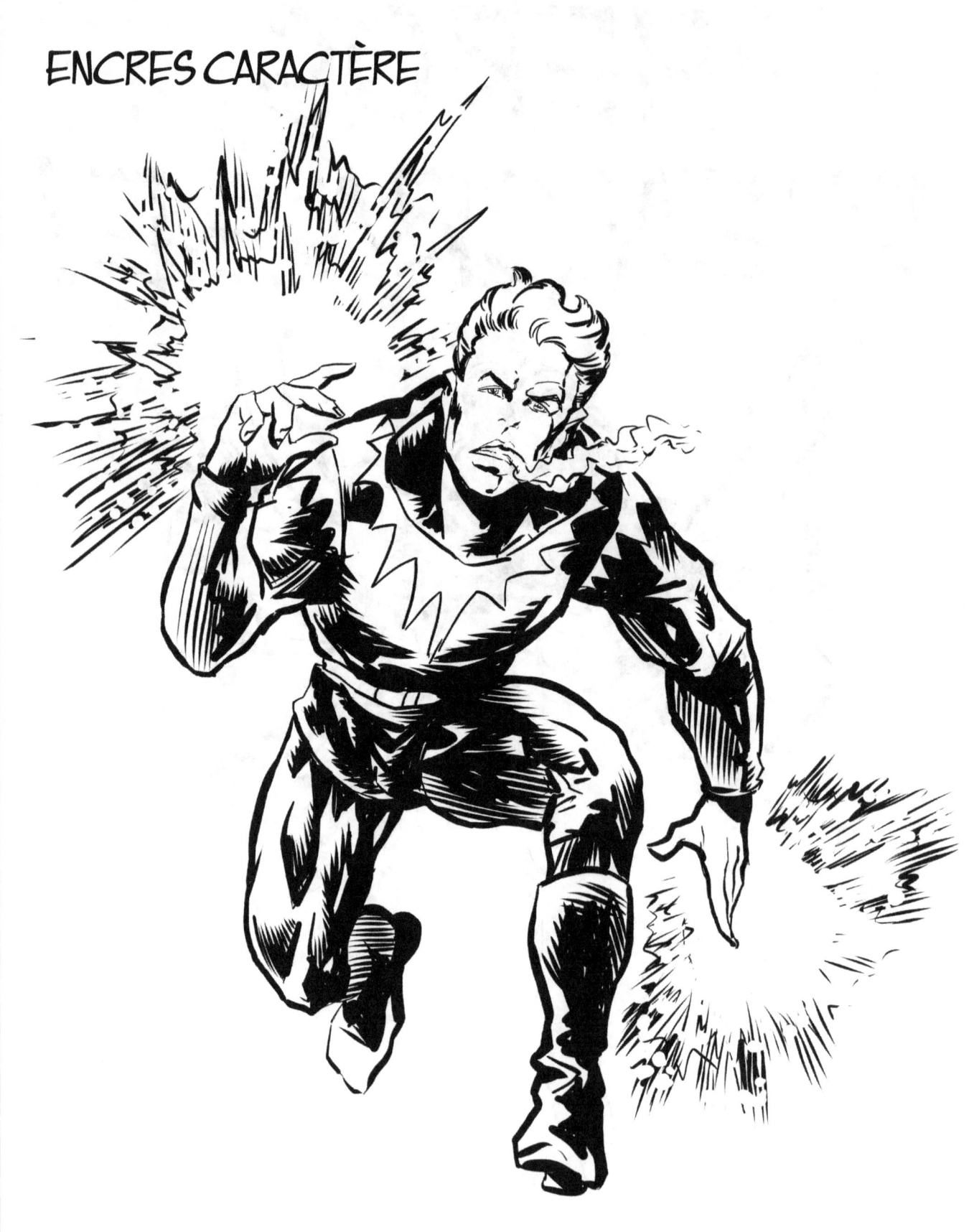

DR. FROST – PRIZE

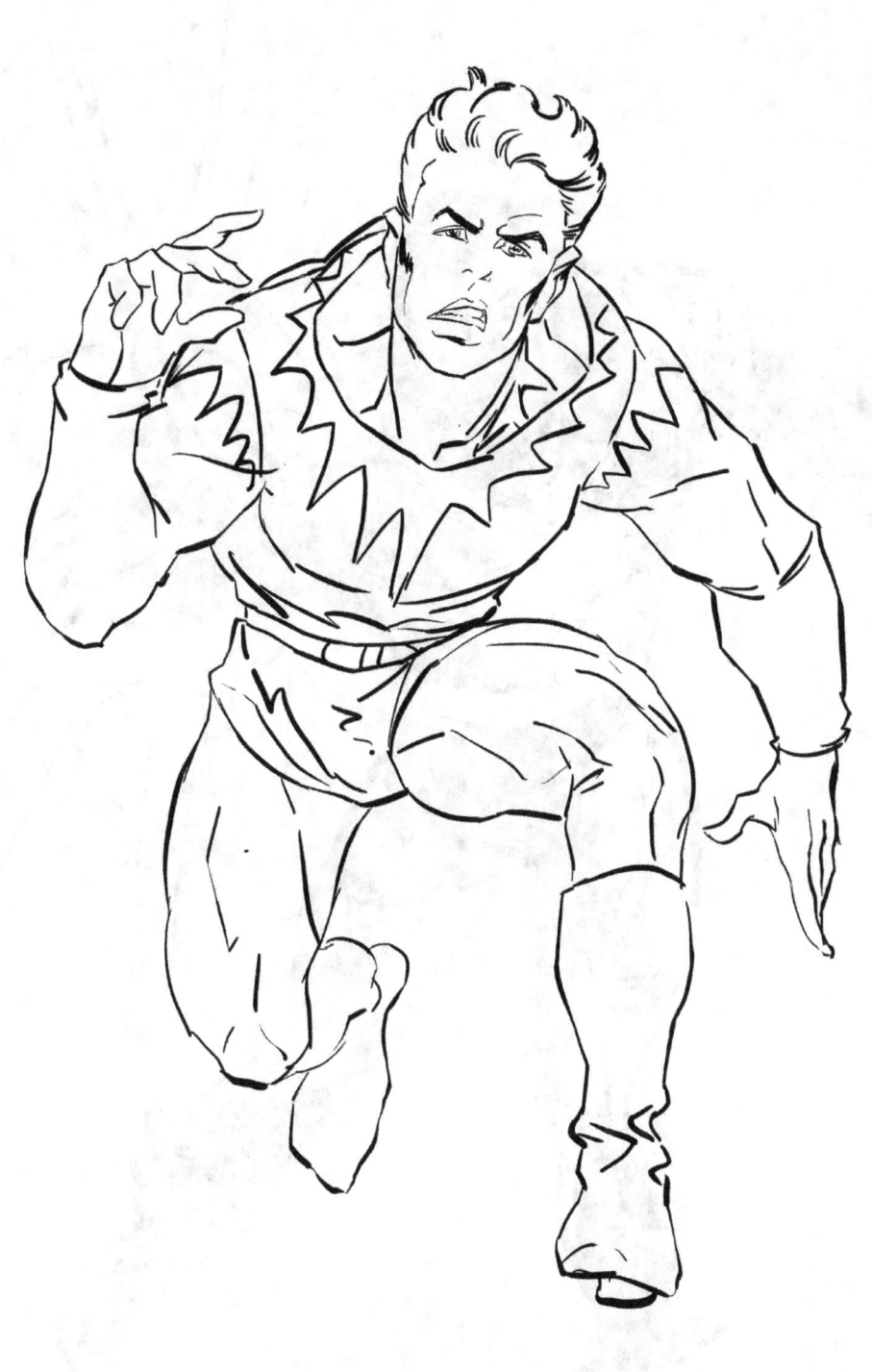

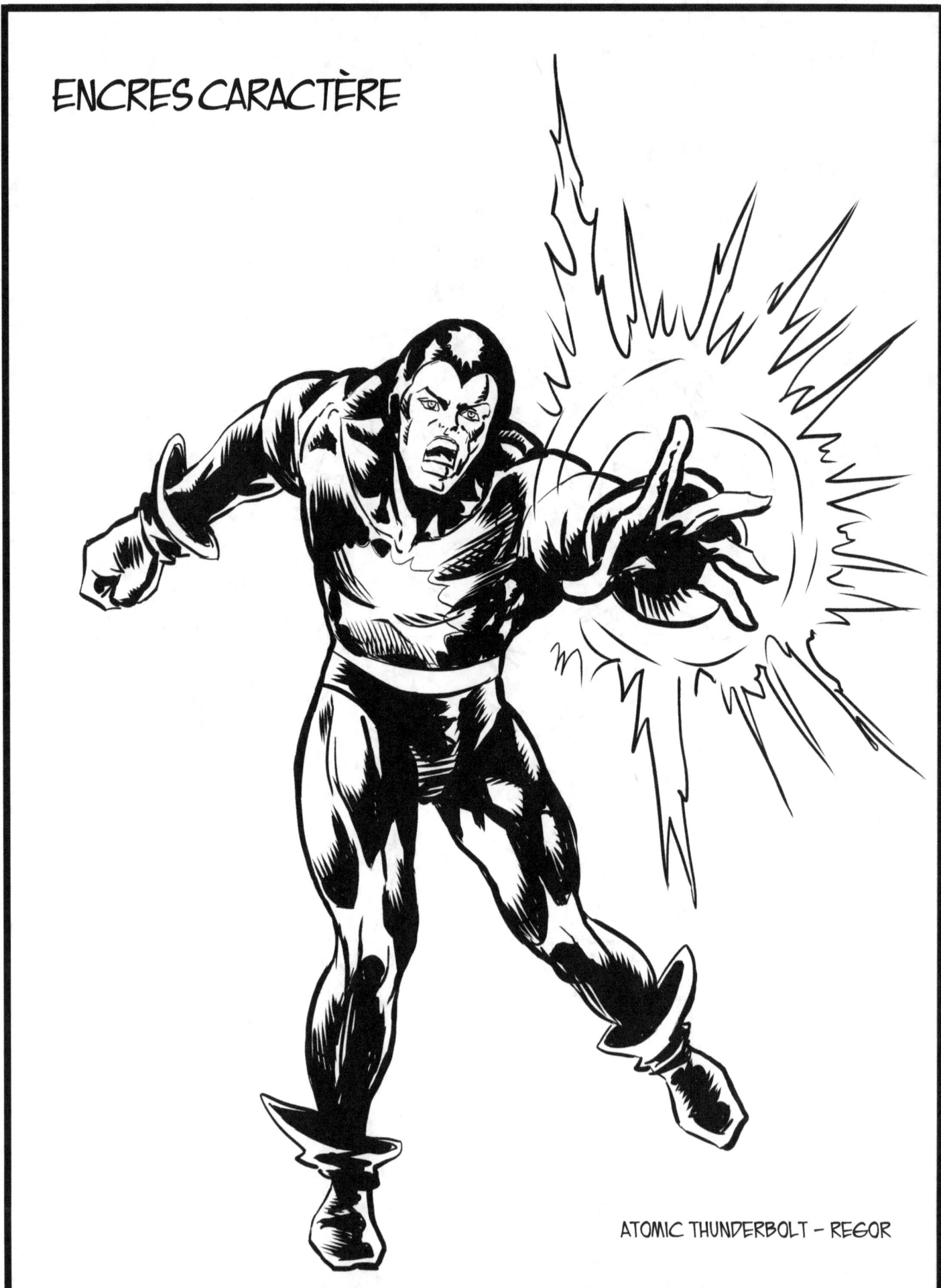

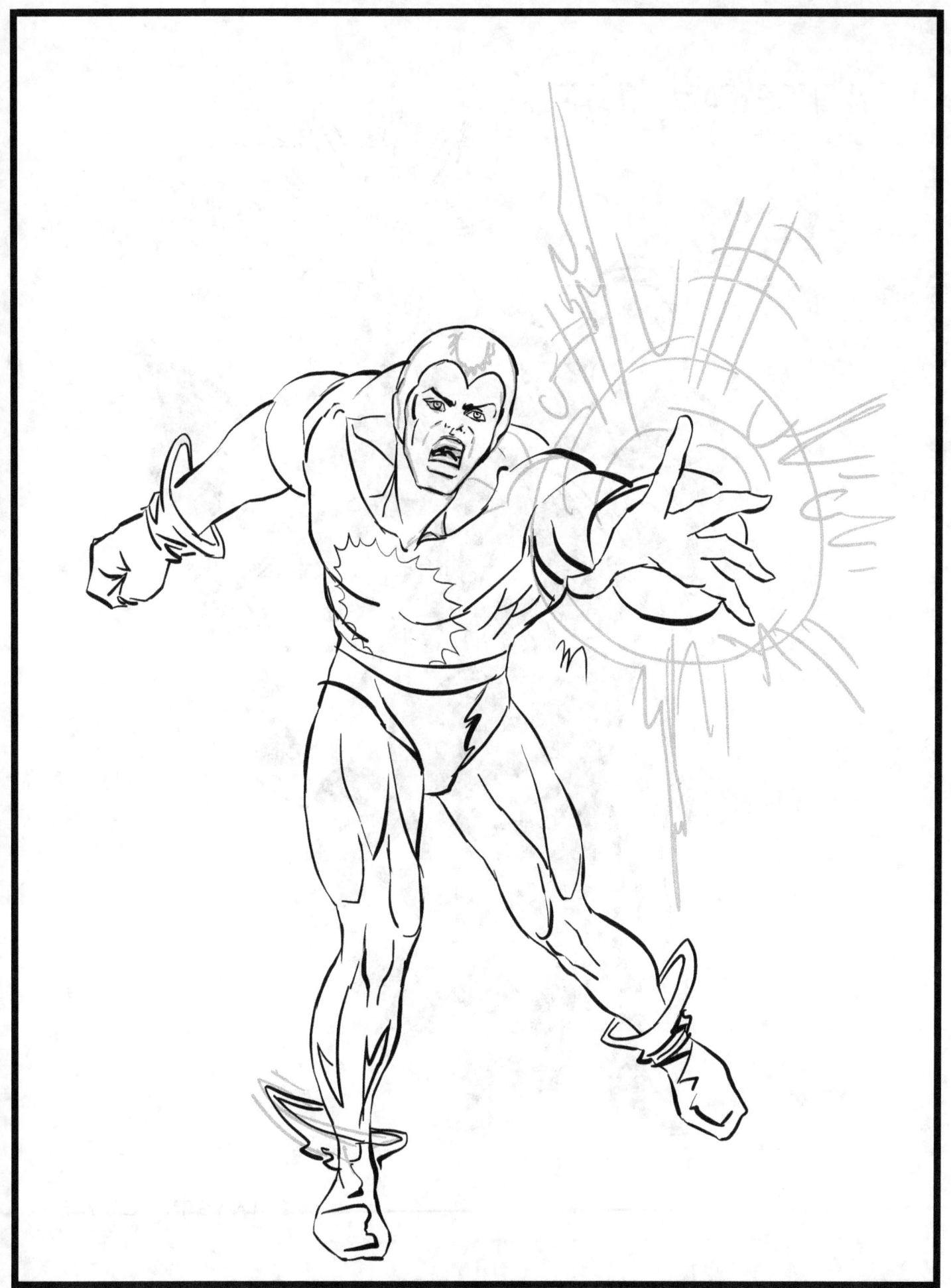

ENCRES CARACTÈRE

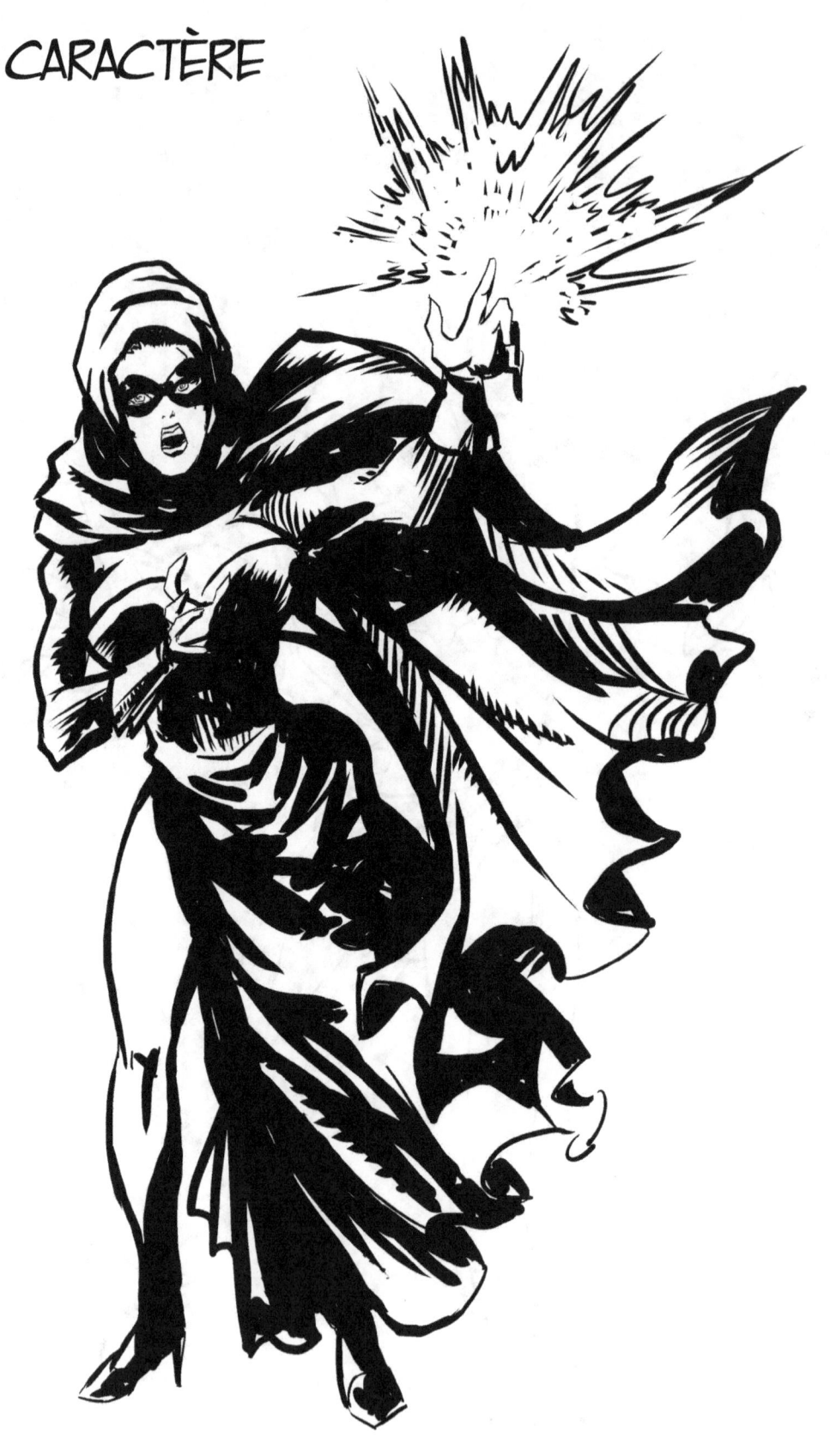

LADY SATAN - CHESLER

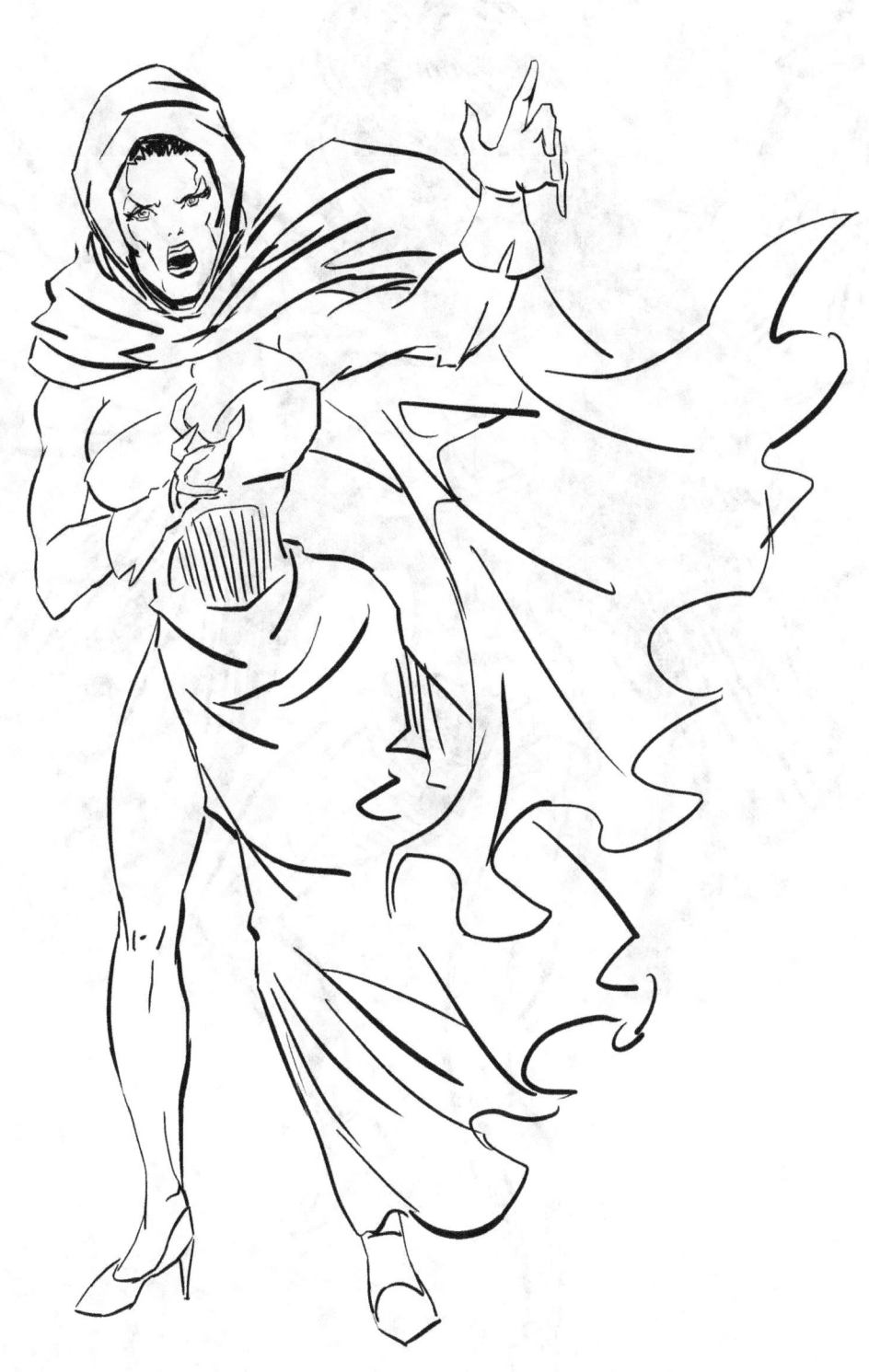

ENCRES CARACTÈRE

YANKEE GIRL - CHESLER

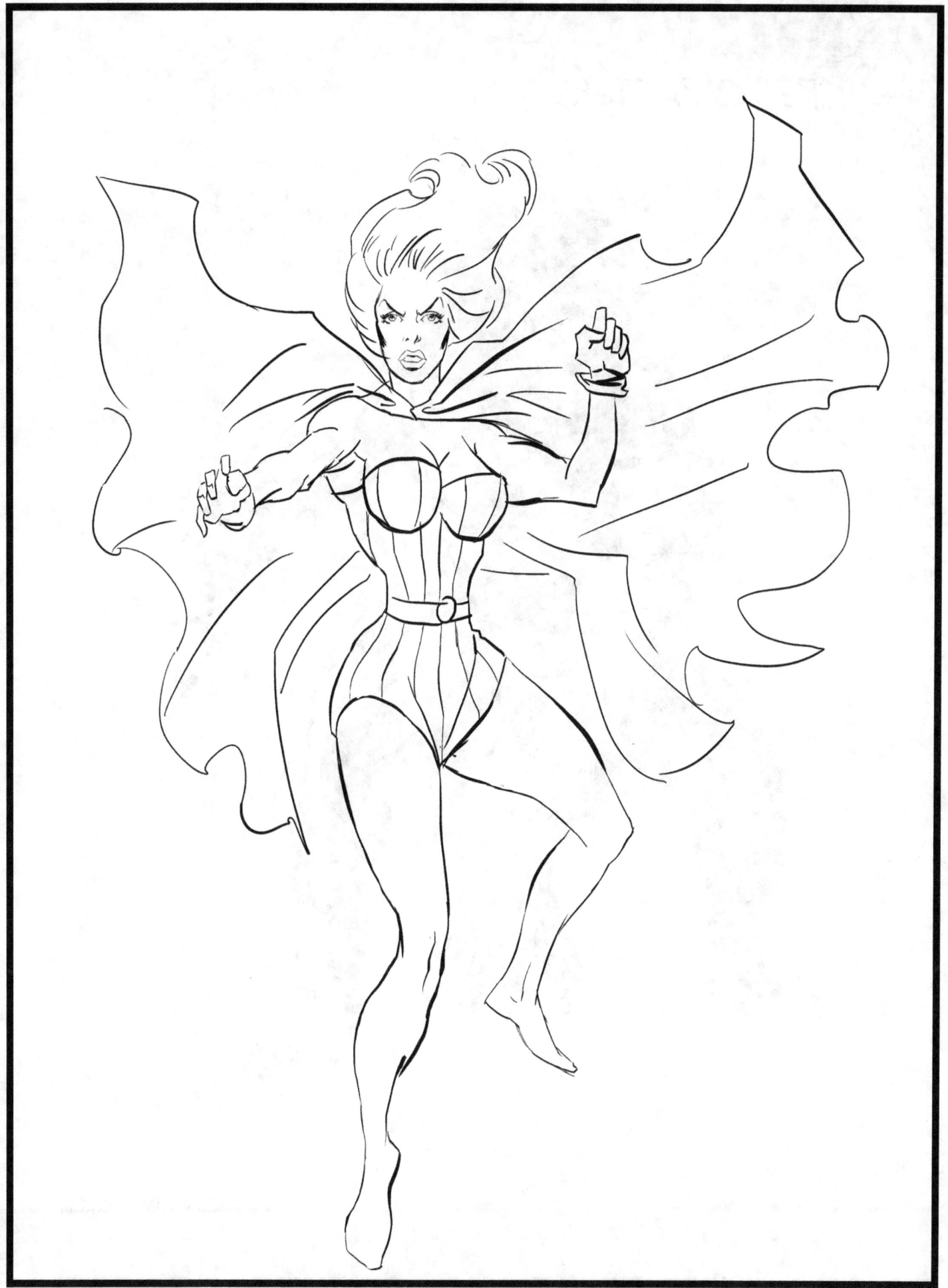

ENCRES CARACTÈRE

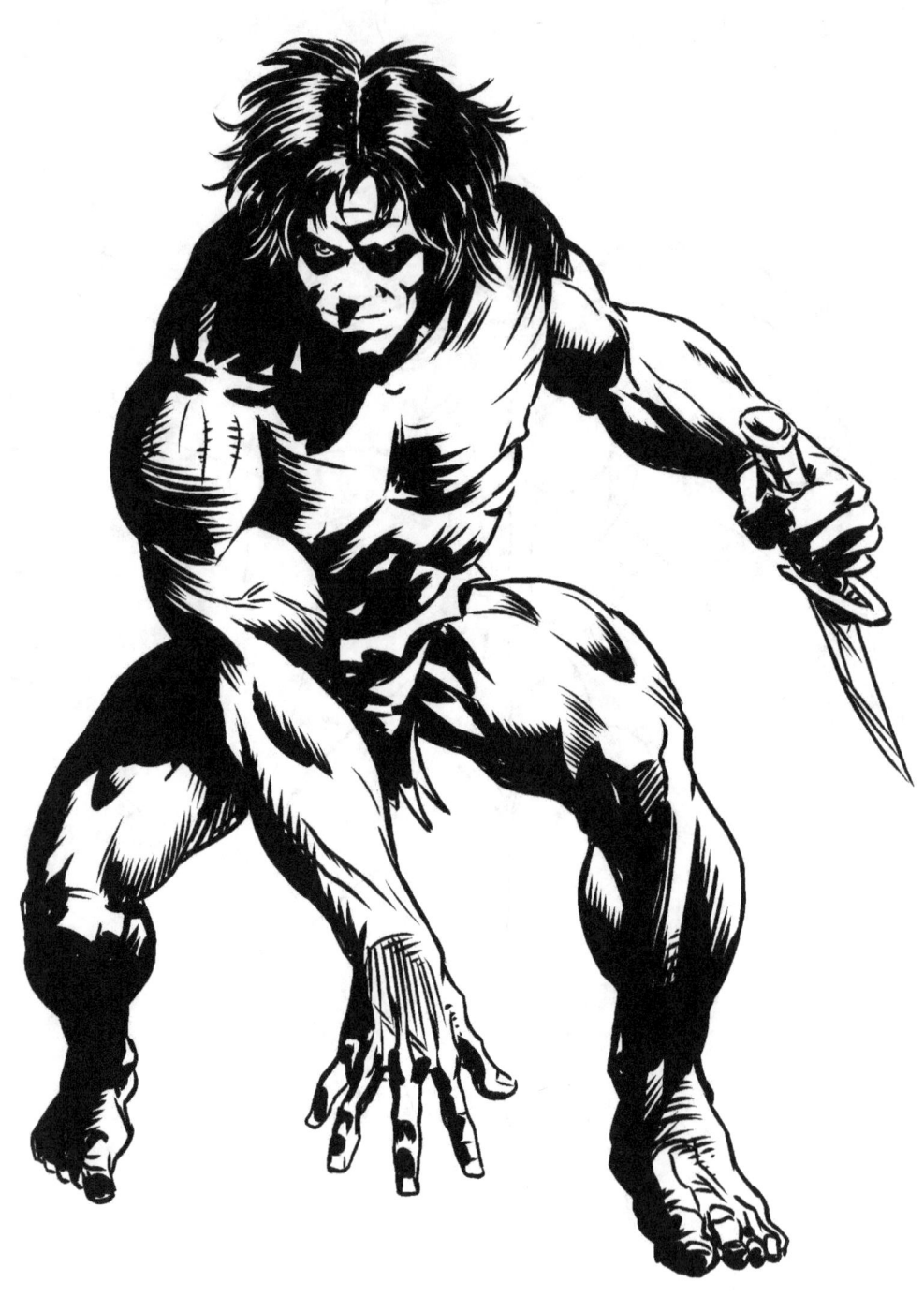

KAZA - AJAX-FARRELL

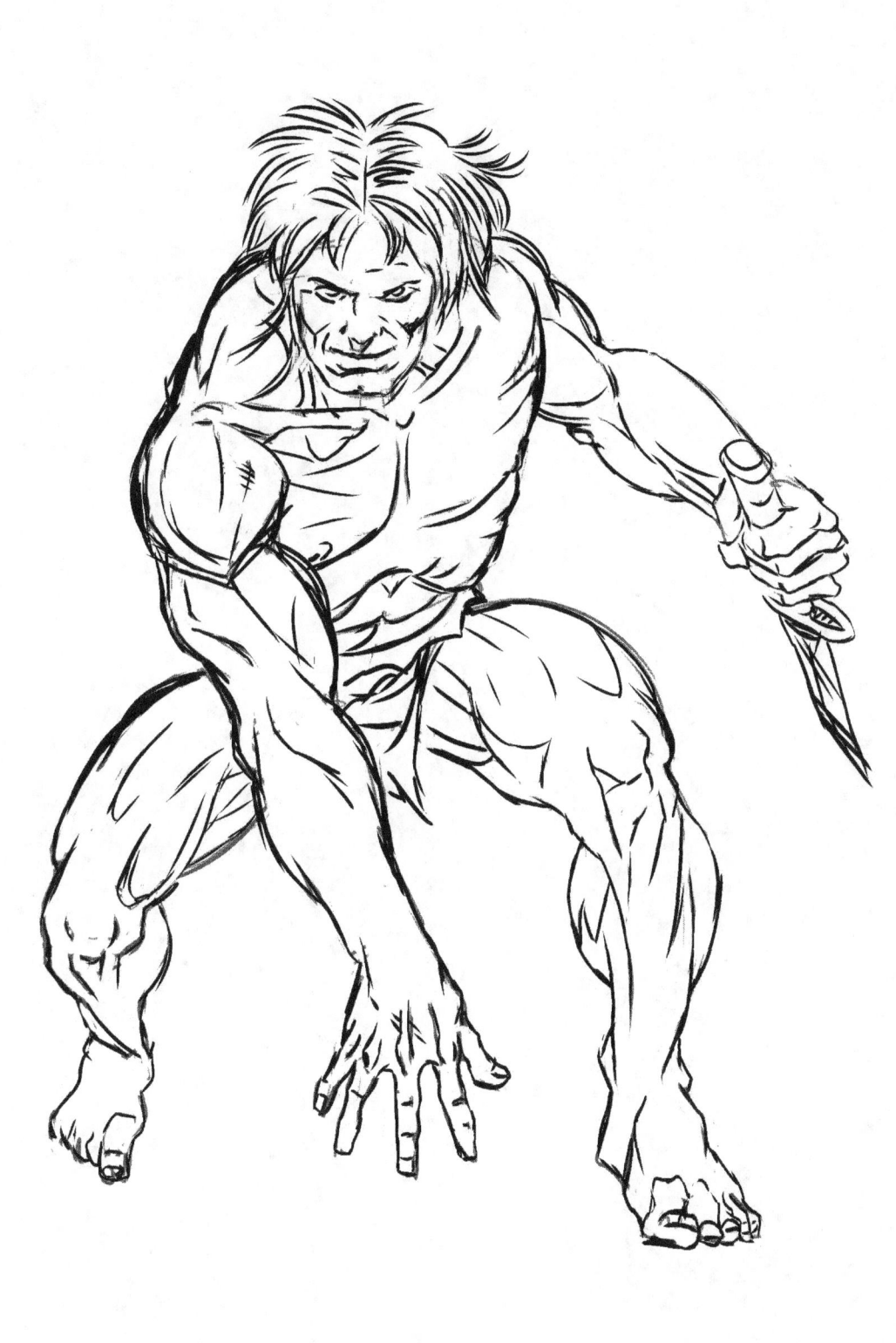

HÉROS DE DESSIN!

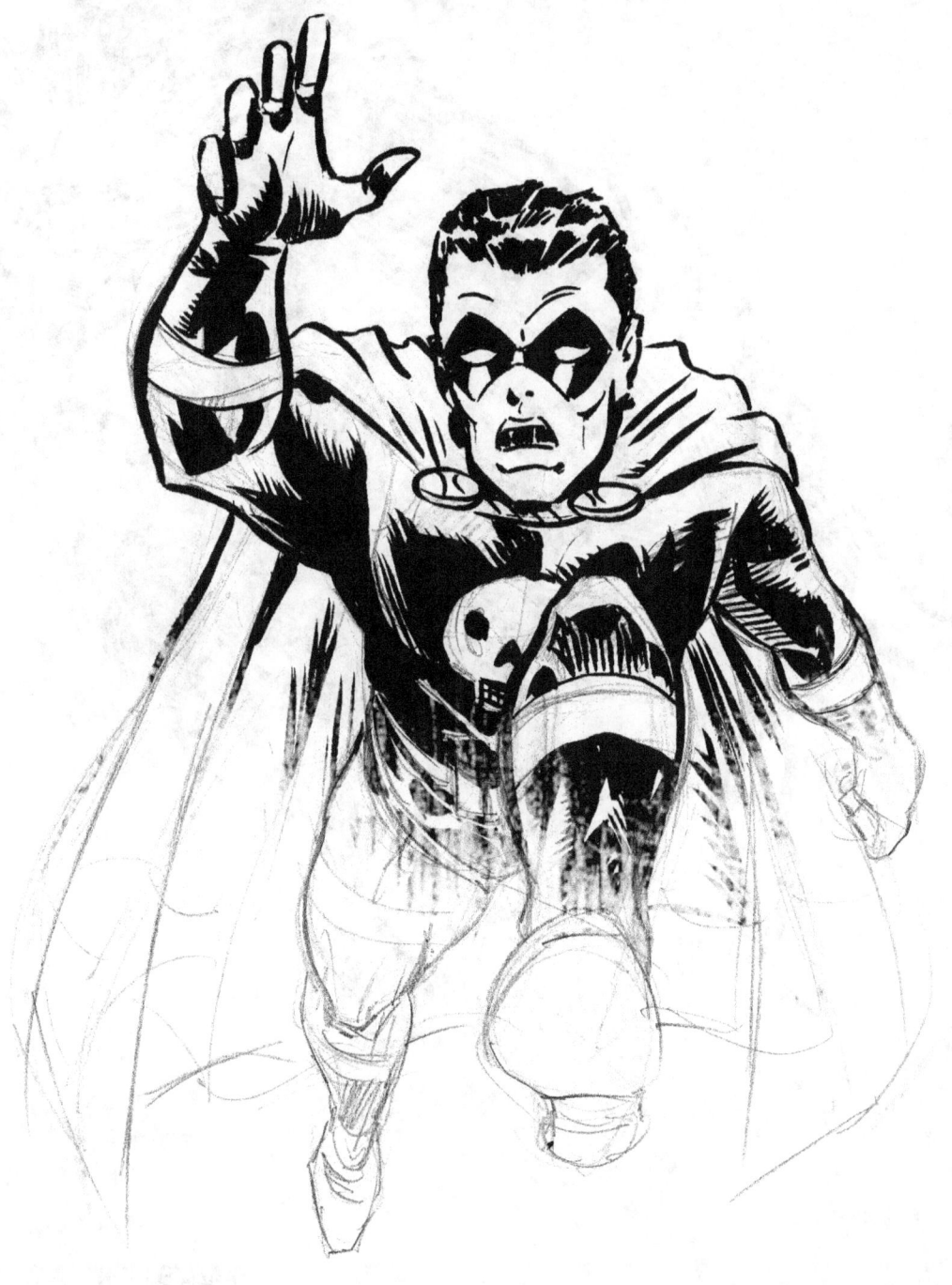

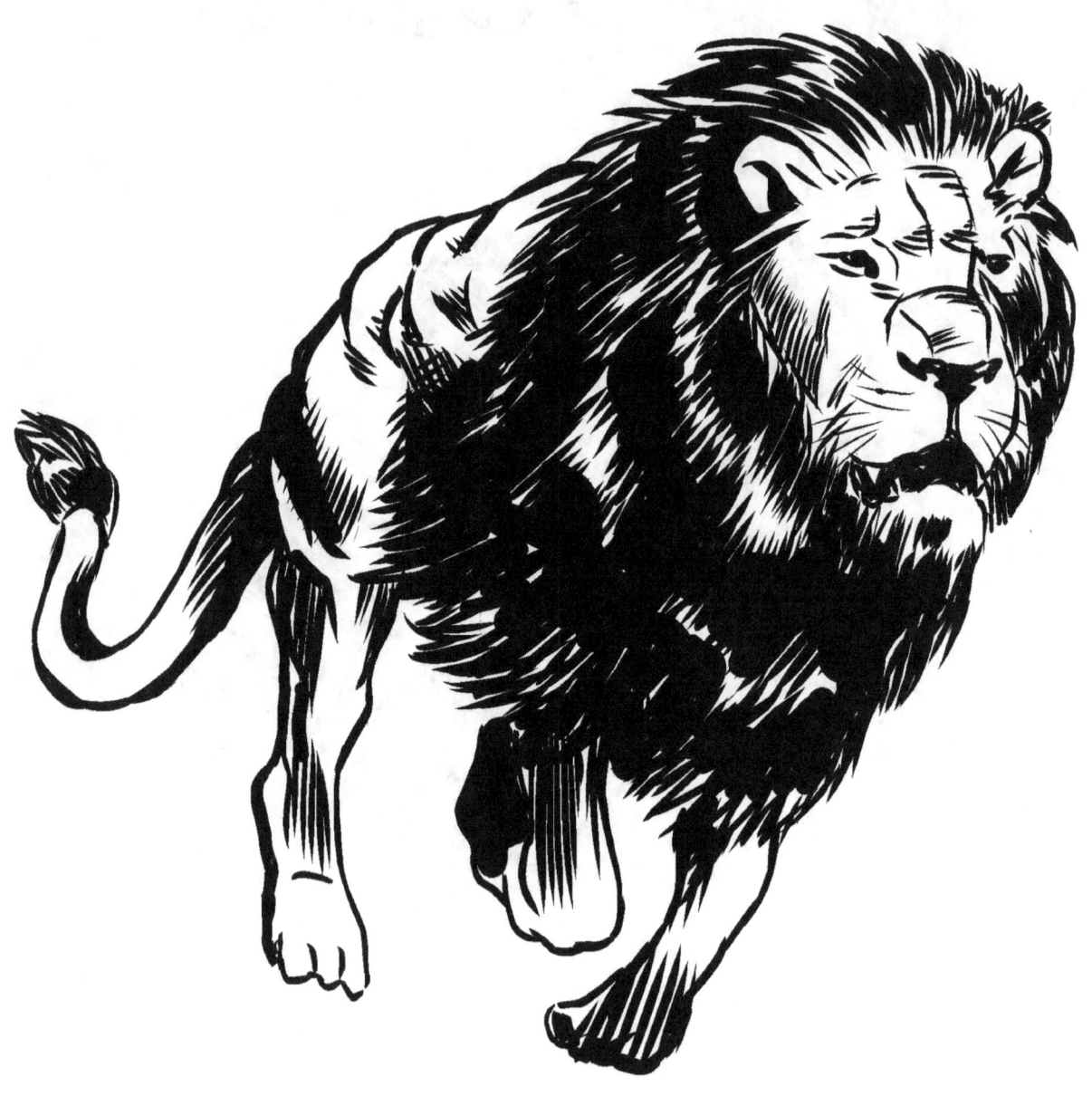

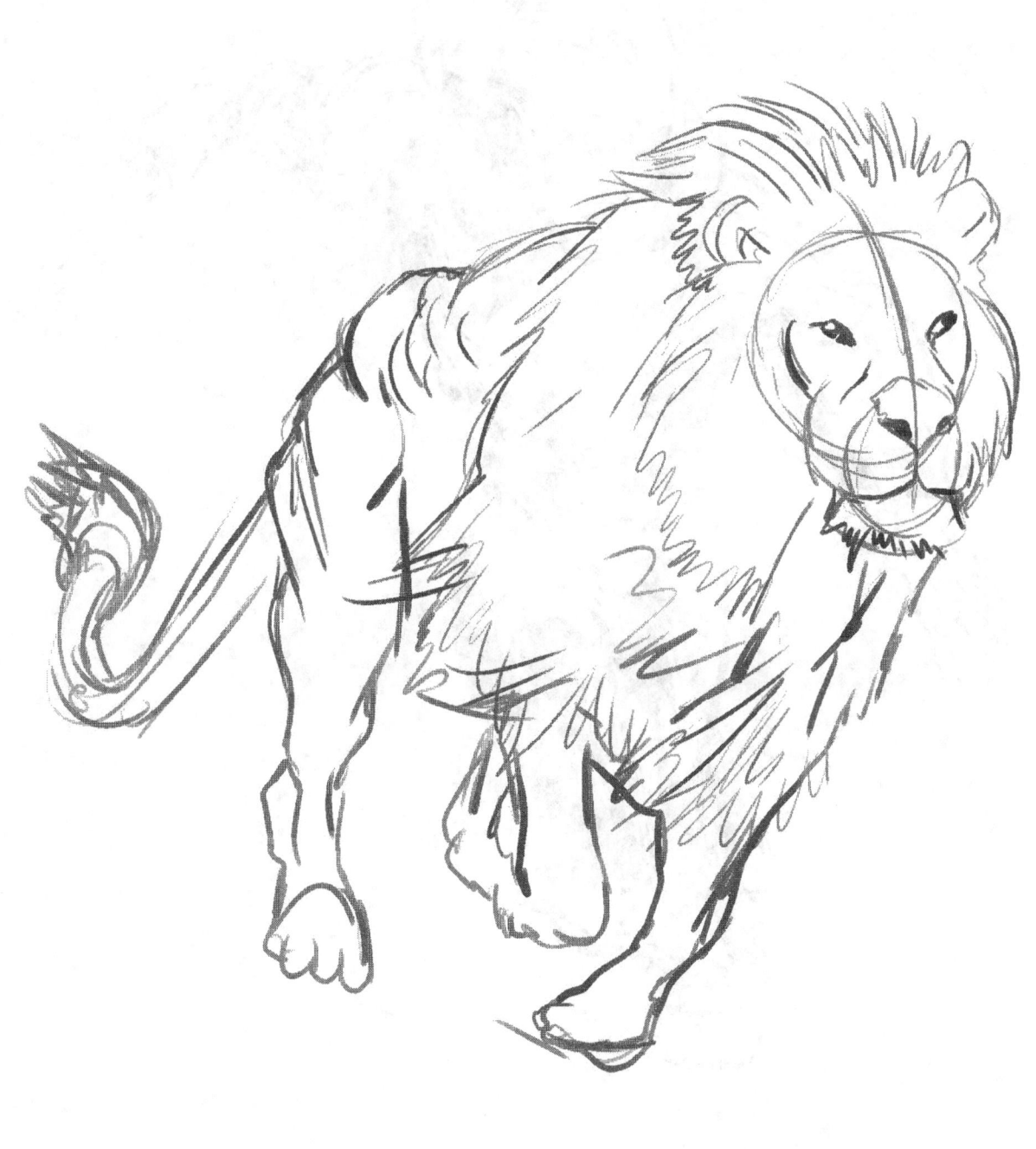

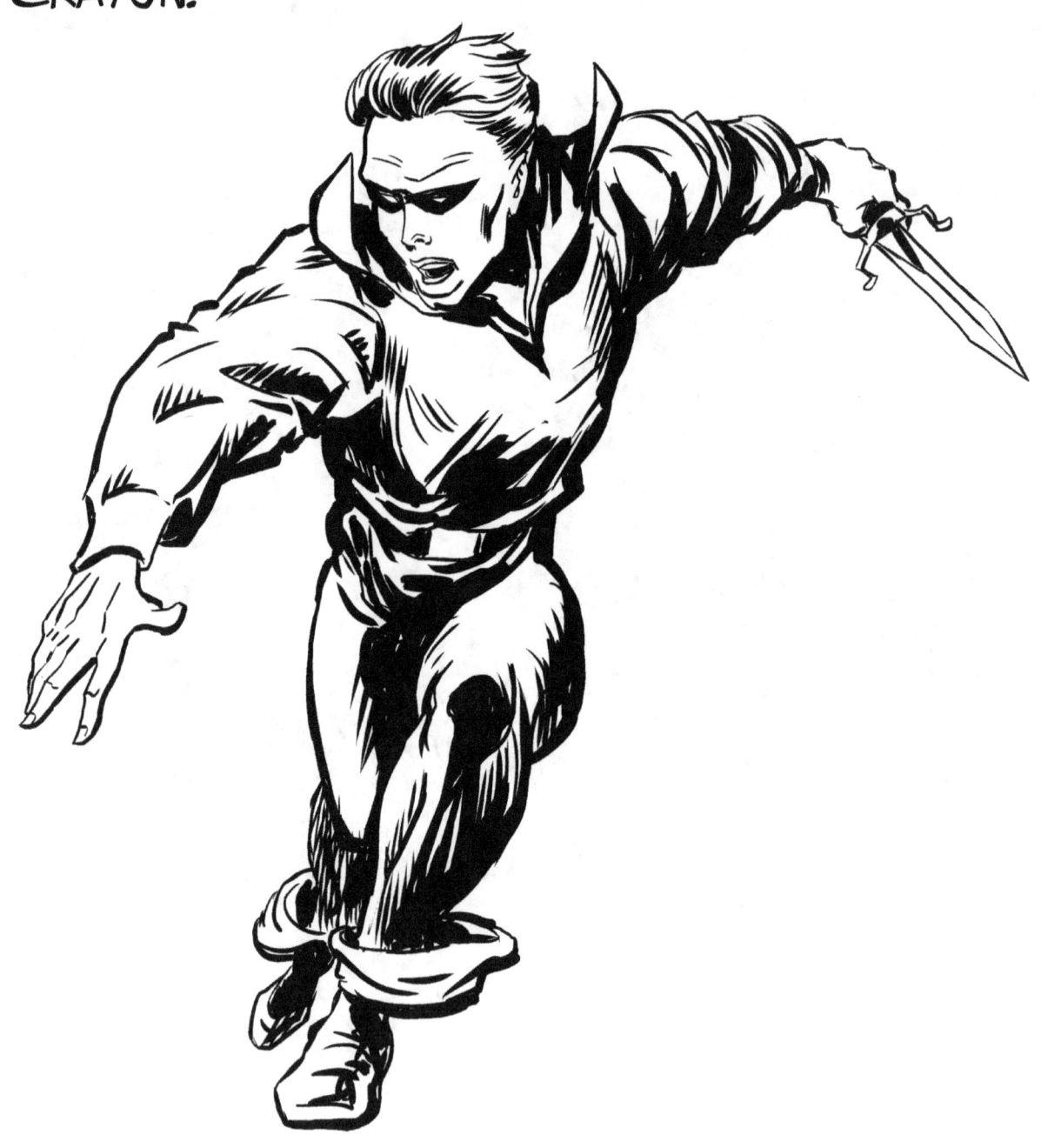

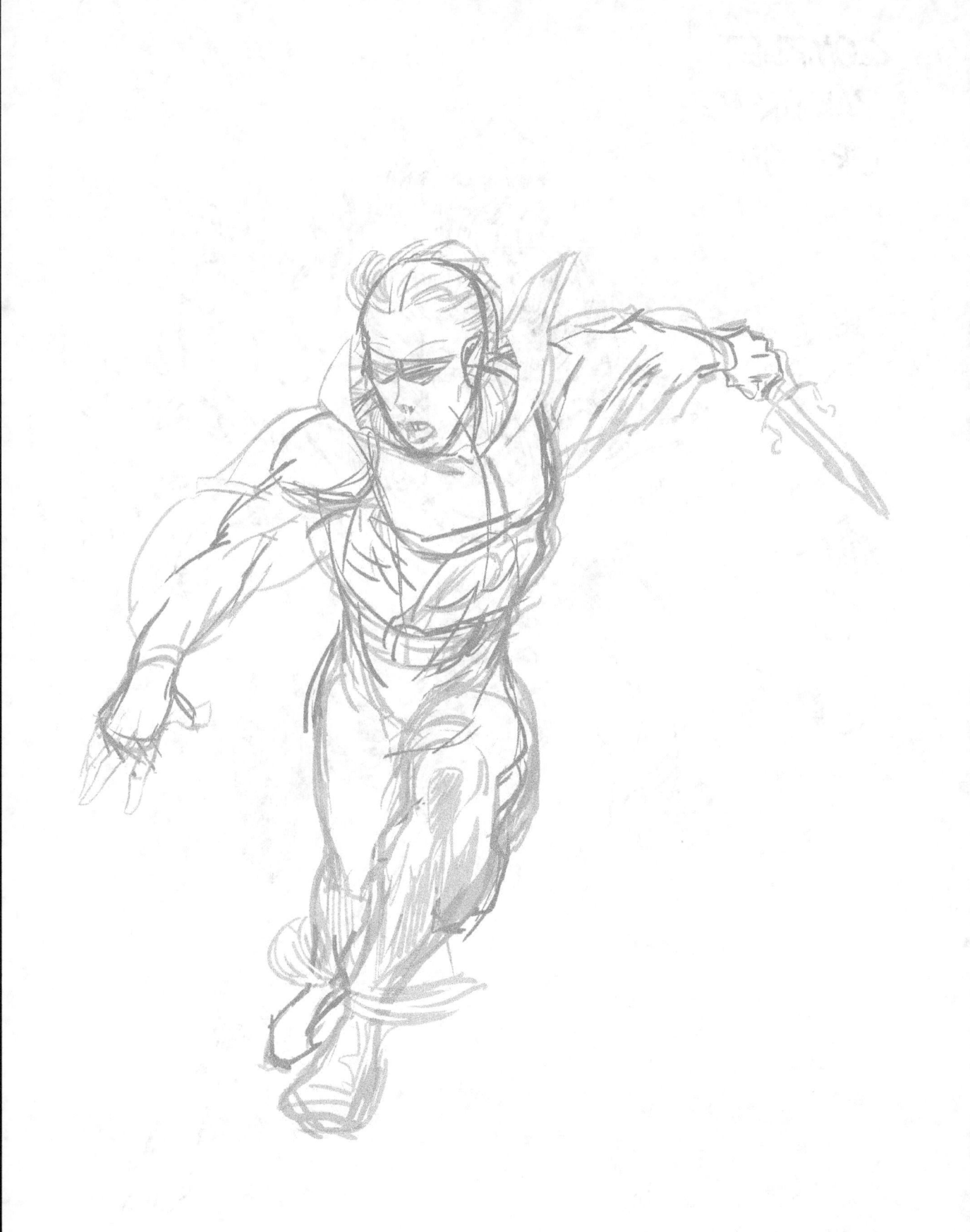

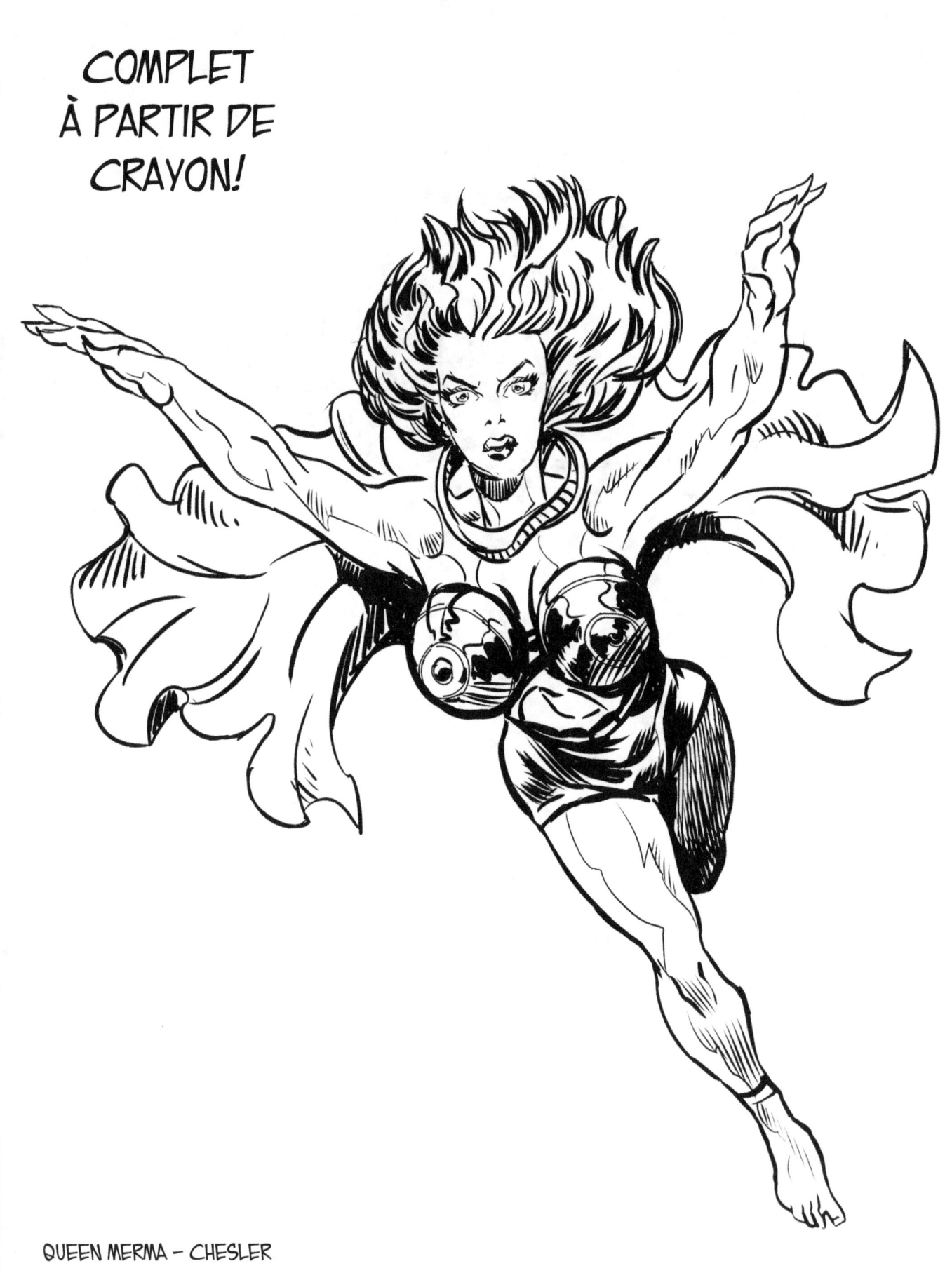

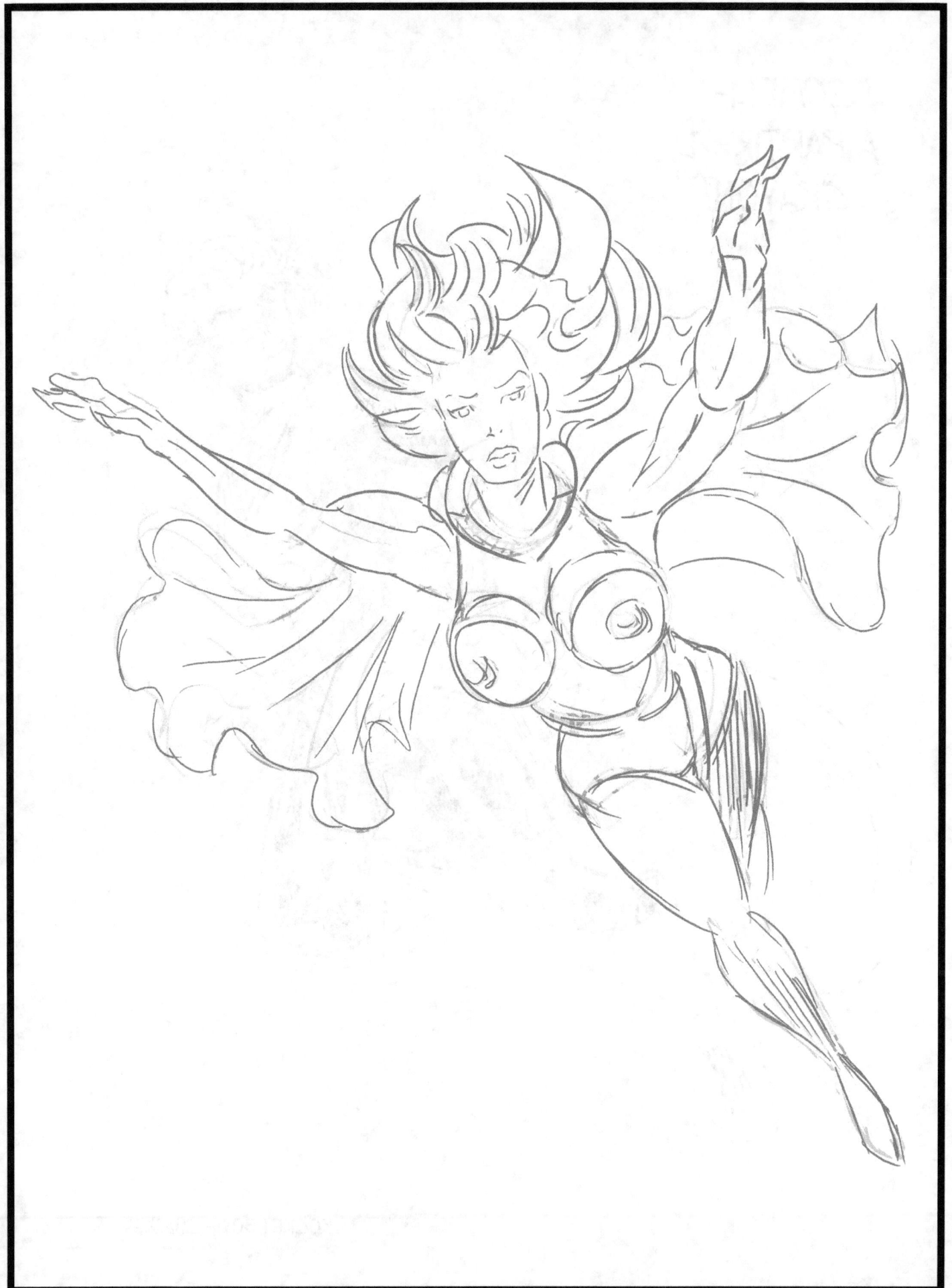

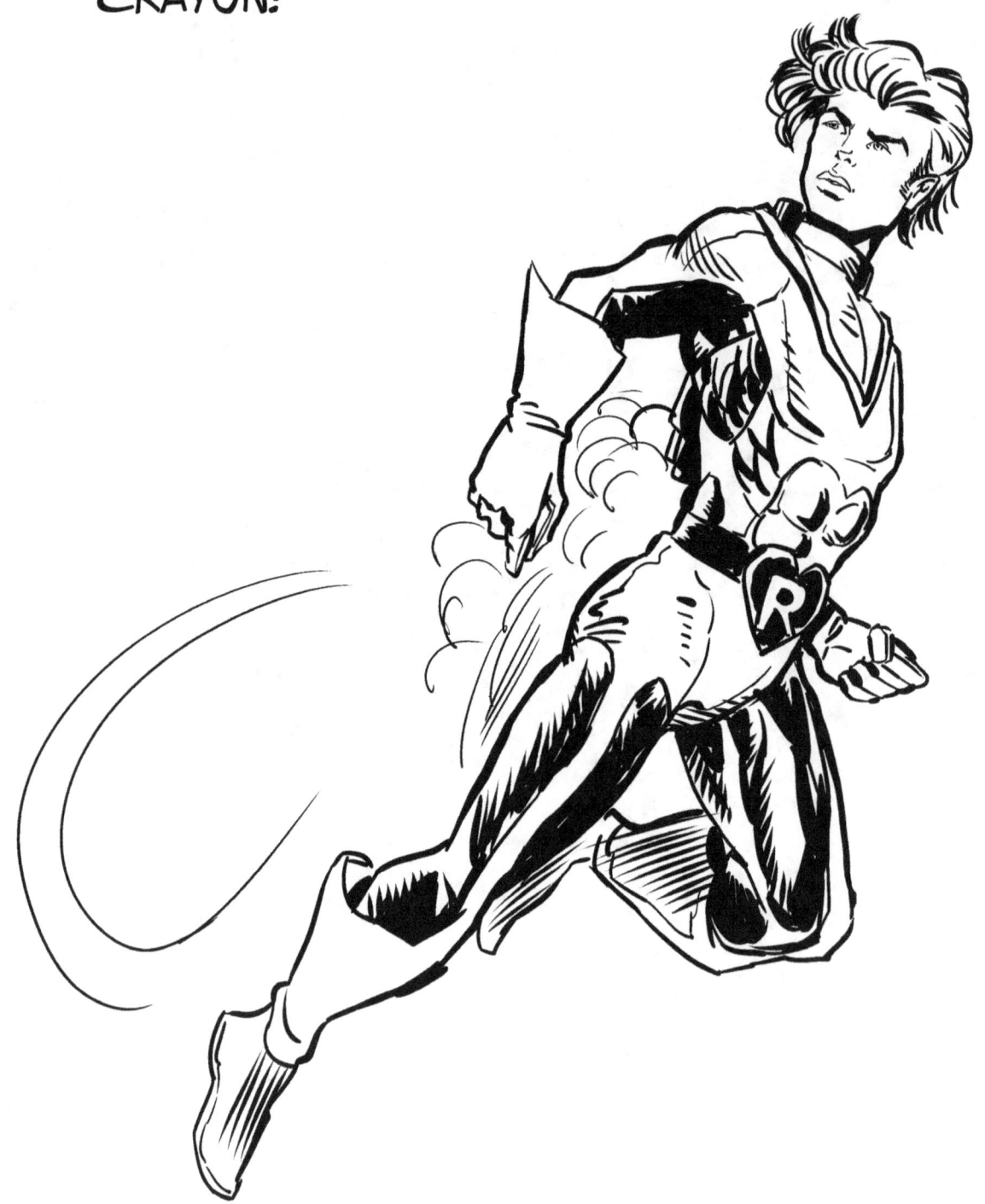

ROCKET BOY – CHESLER

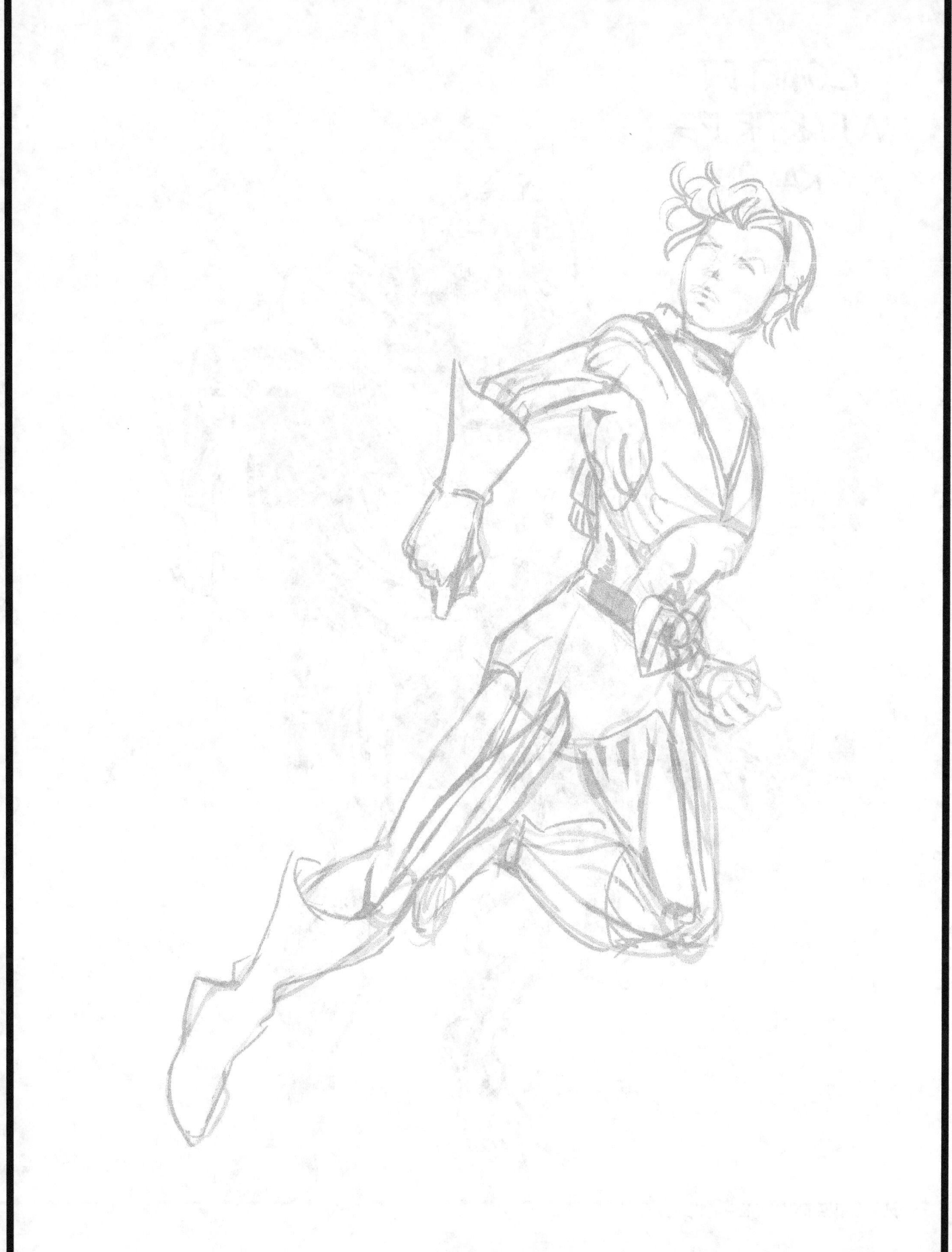

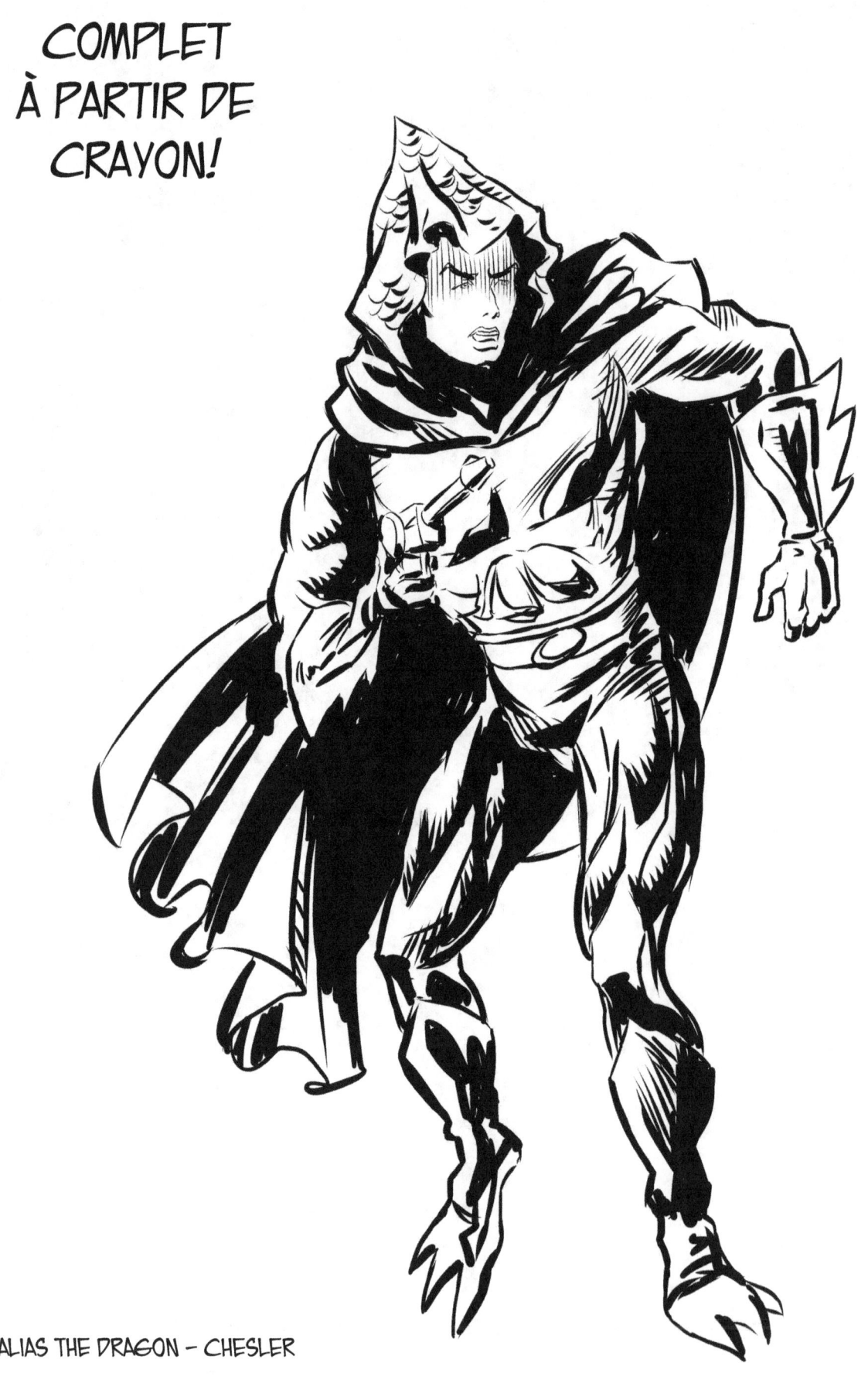

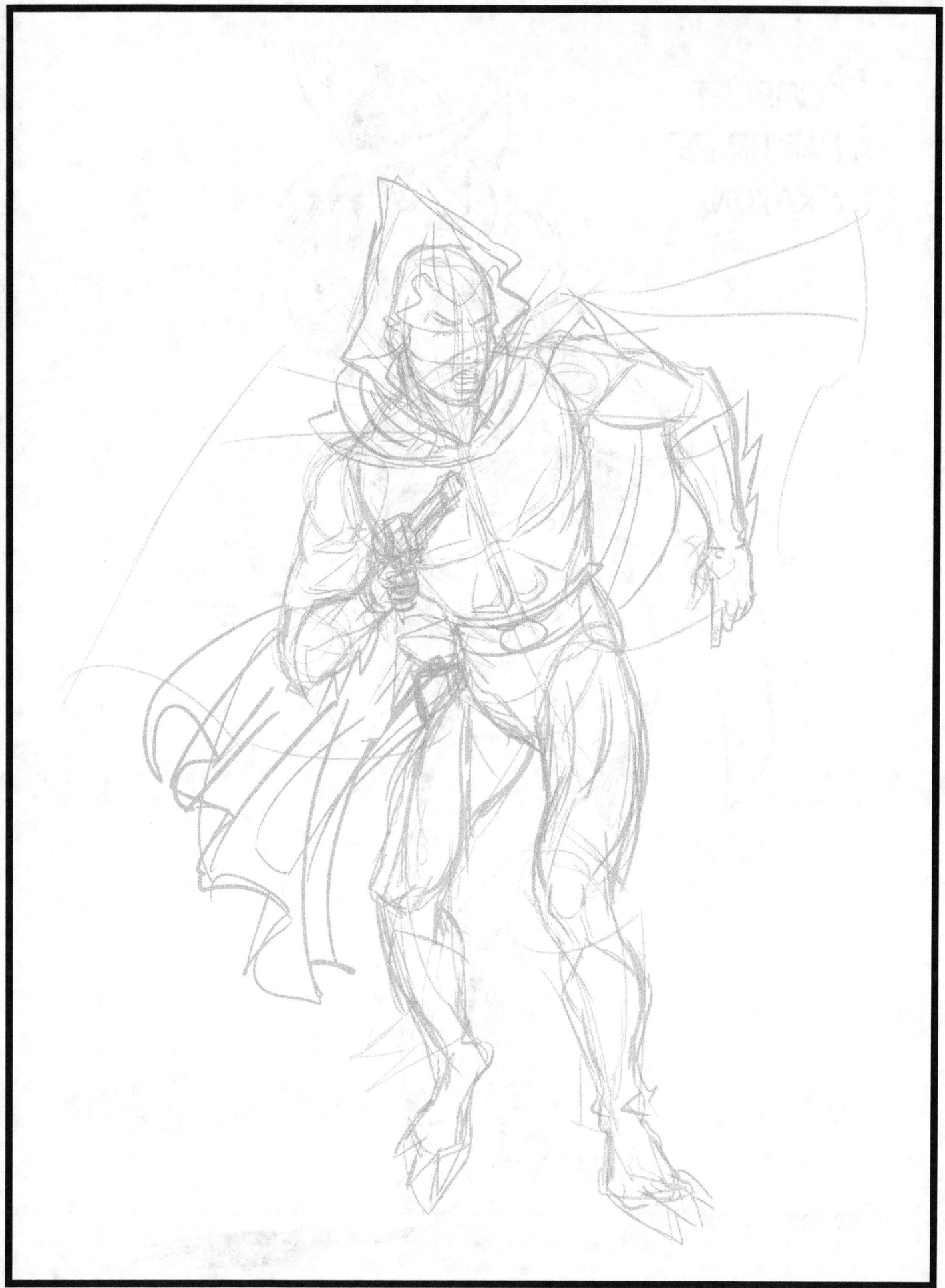

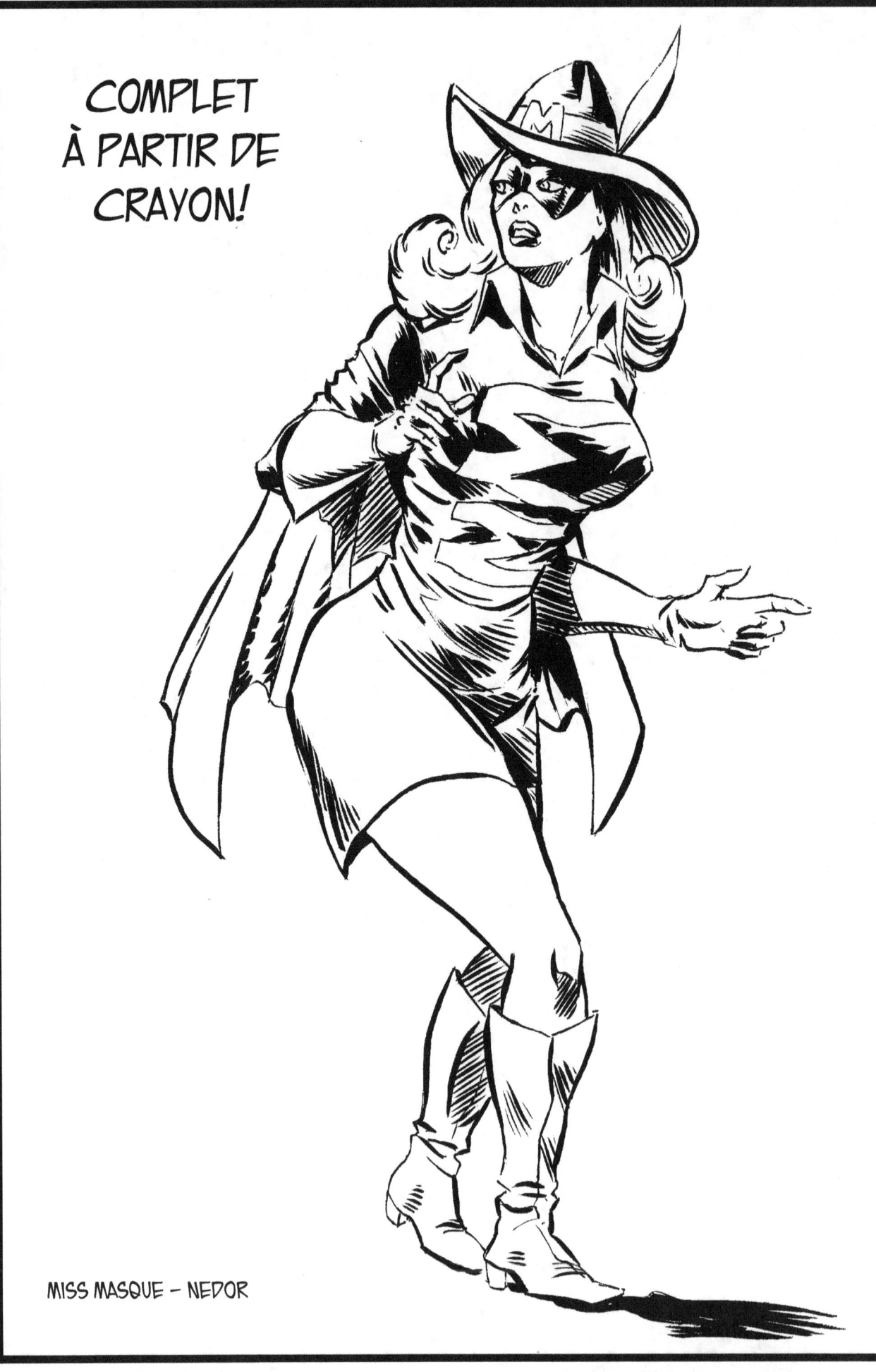

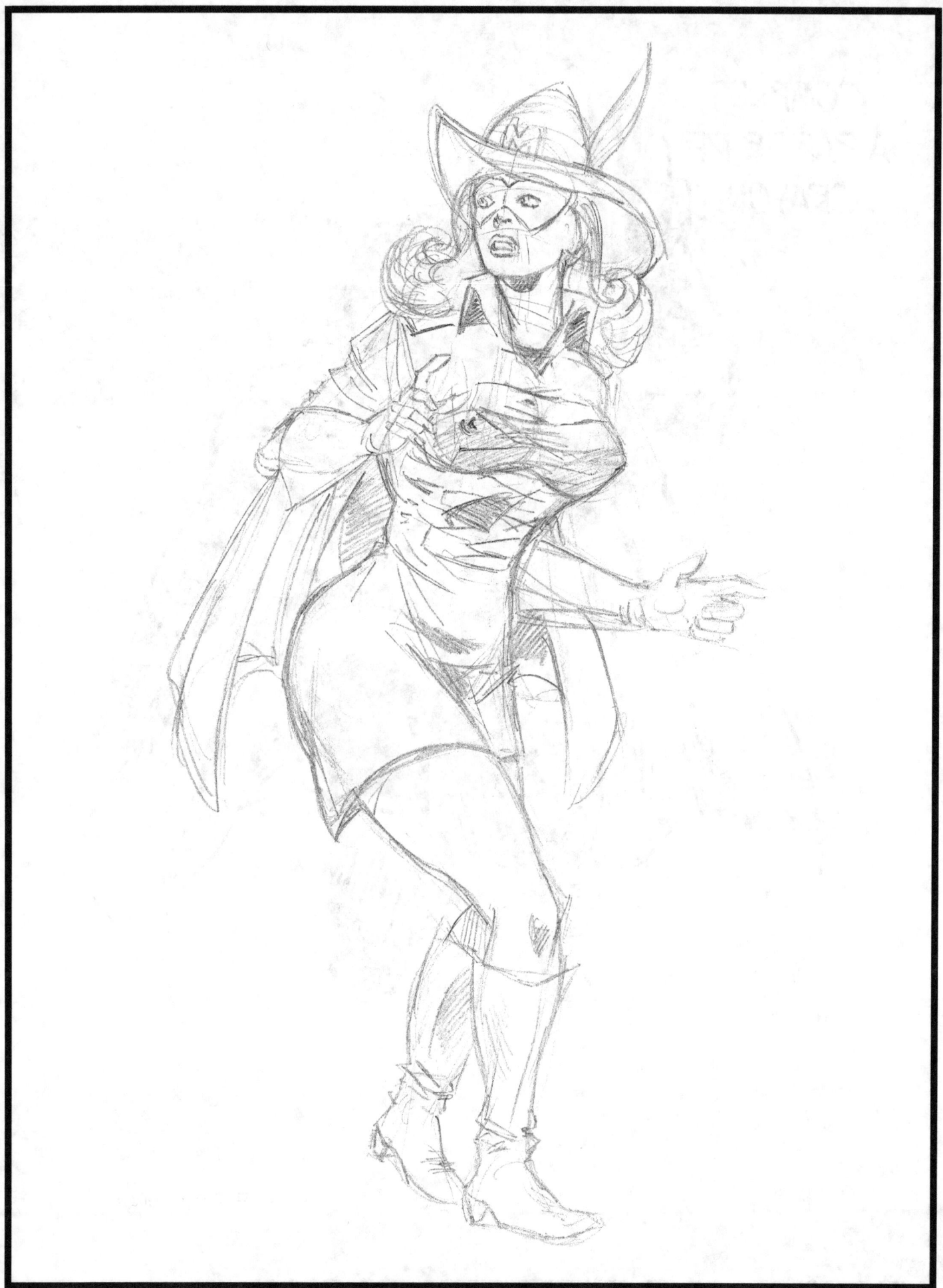

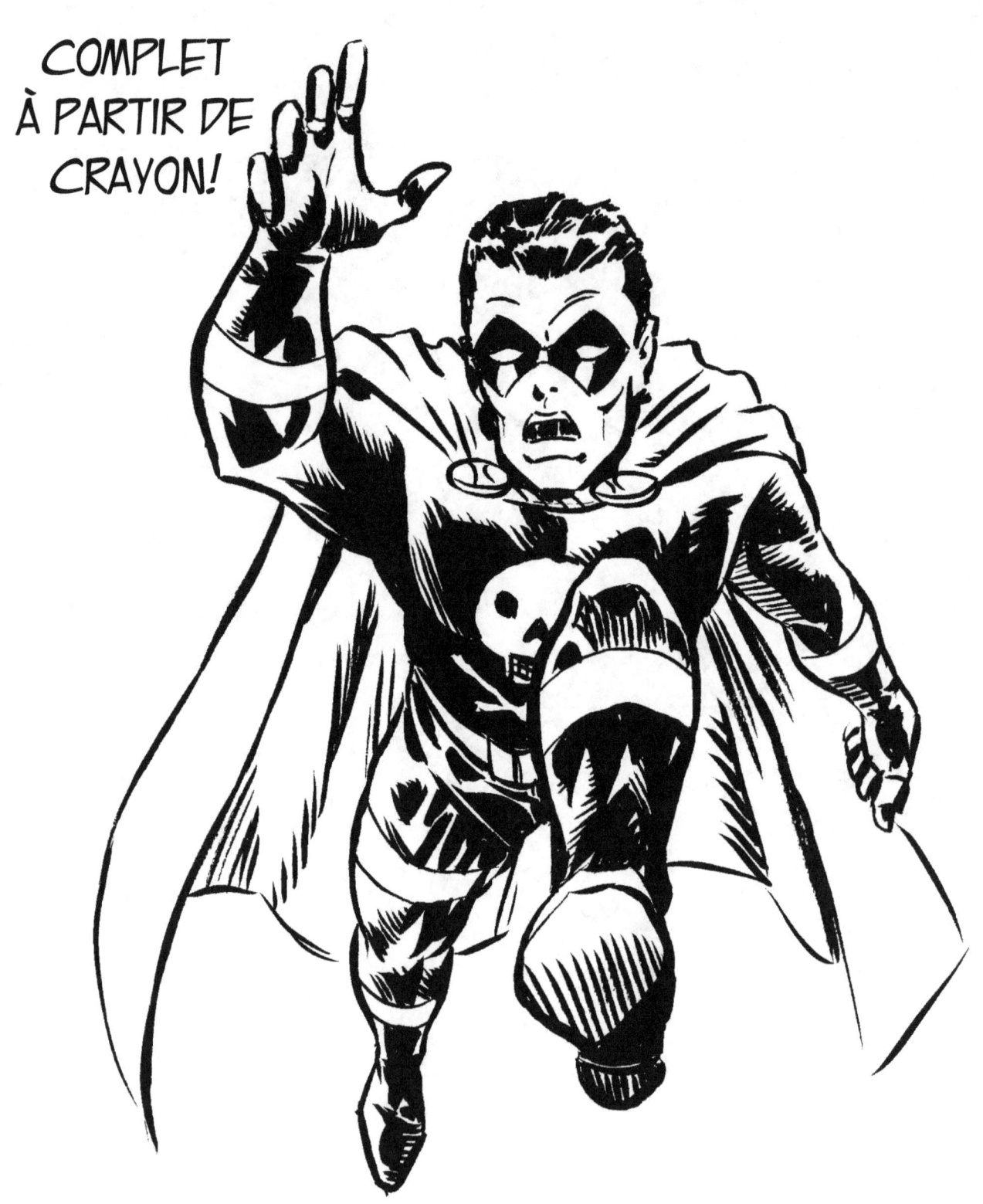

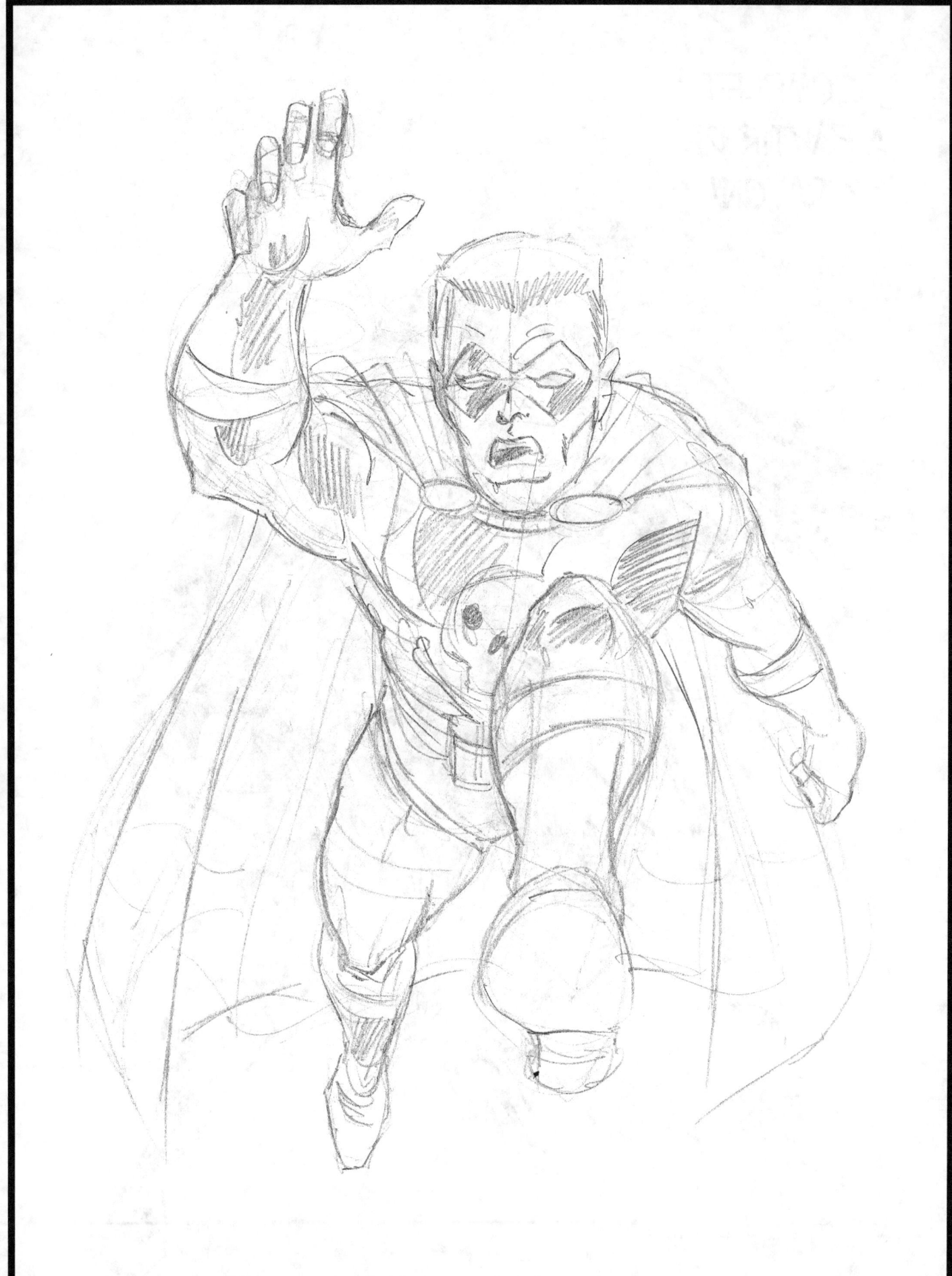

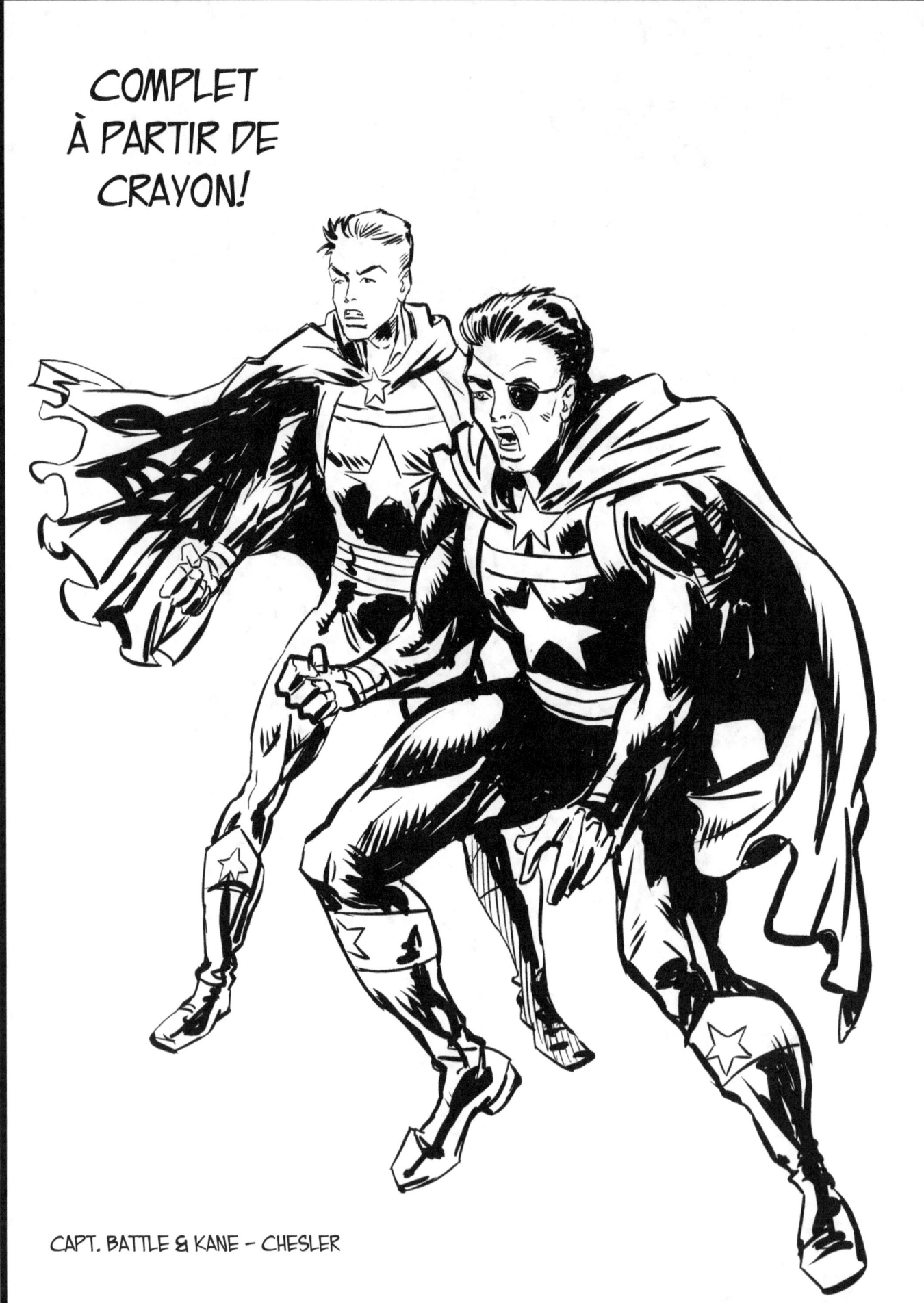

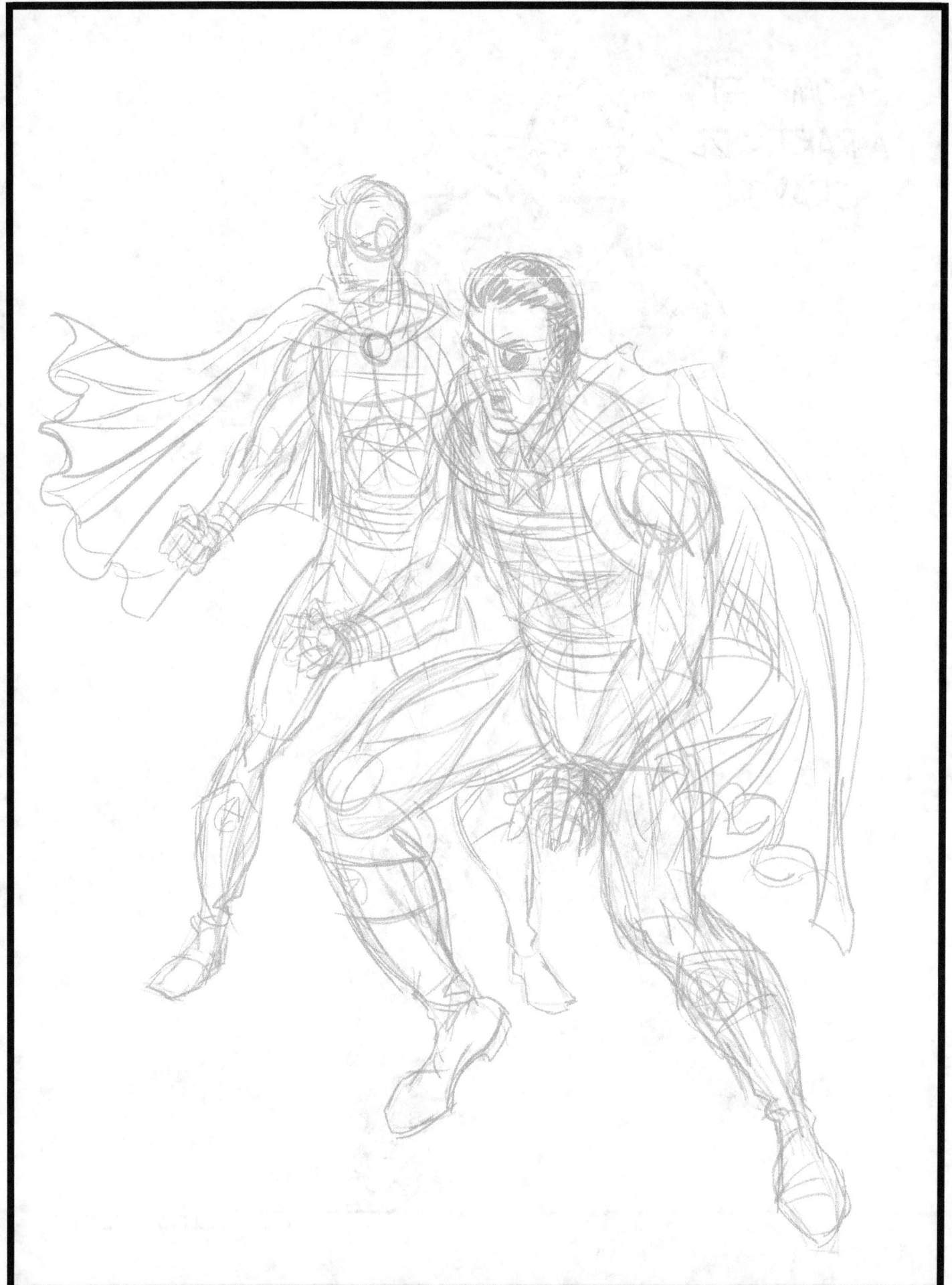

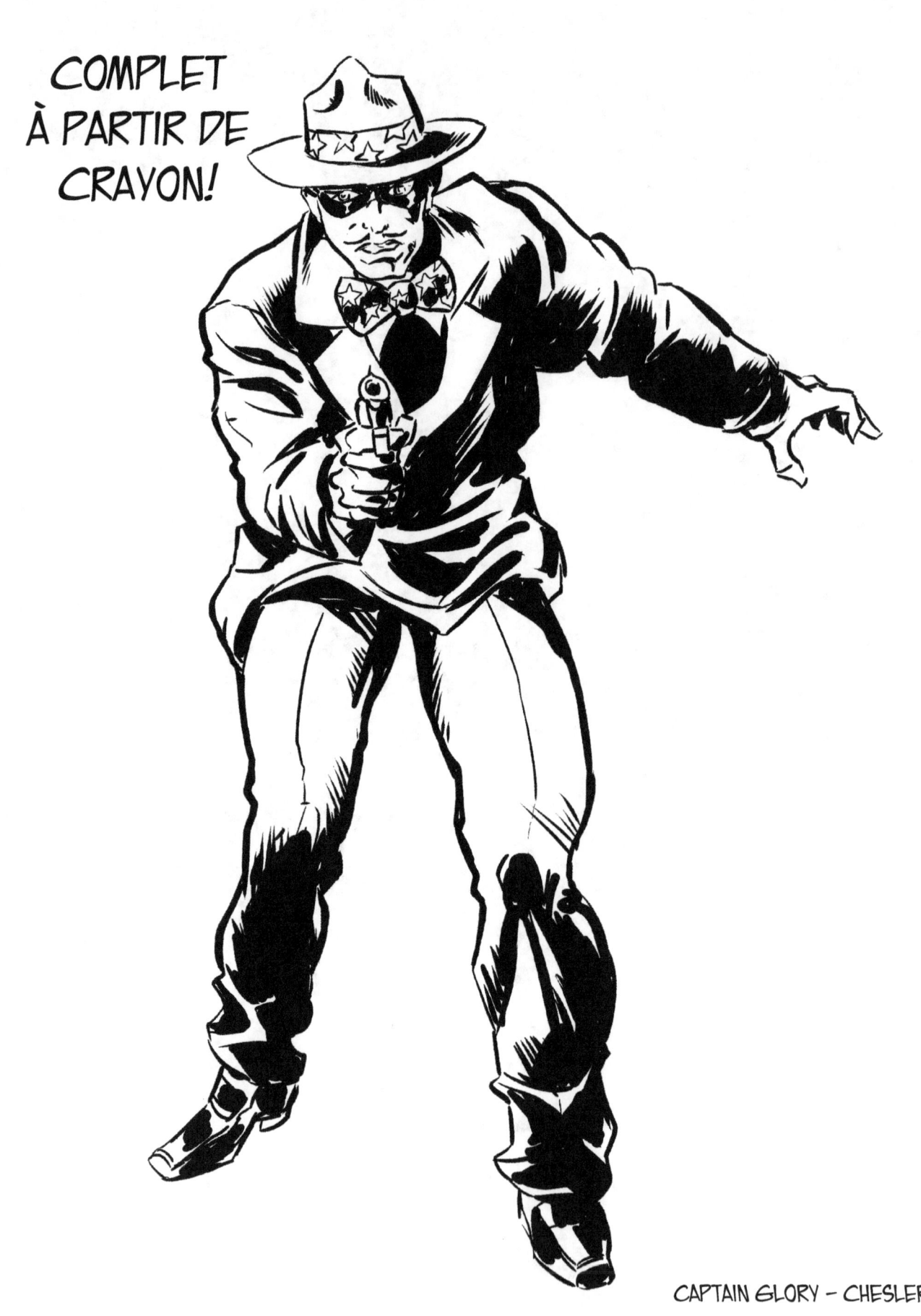

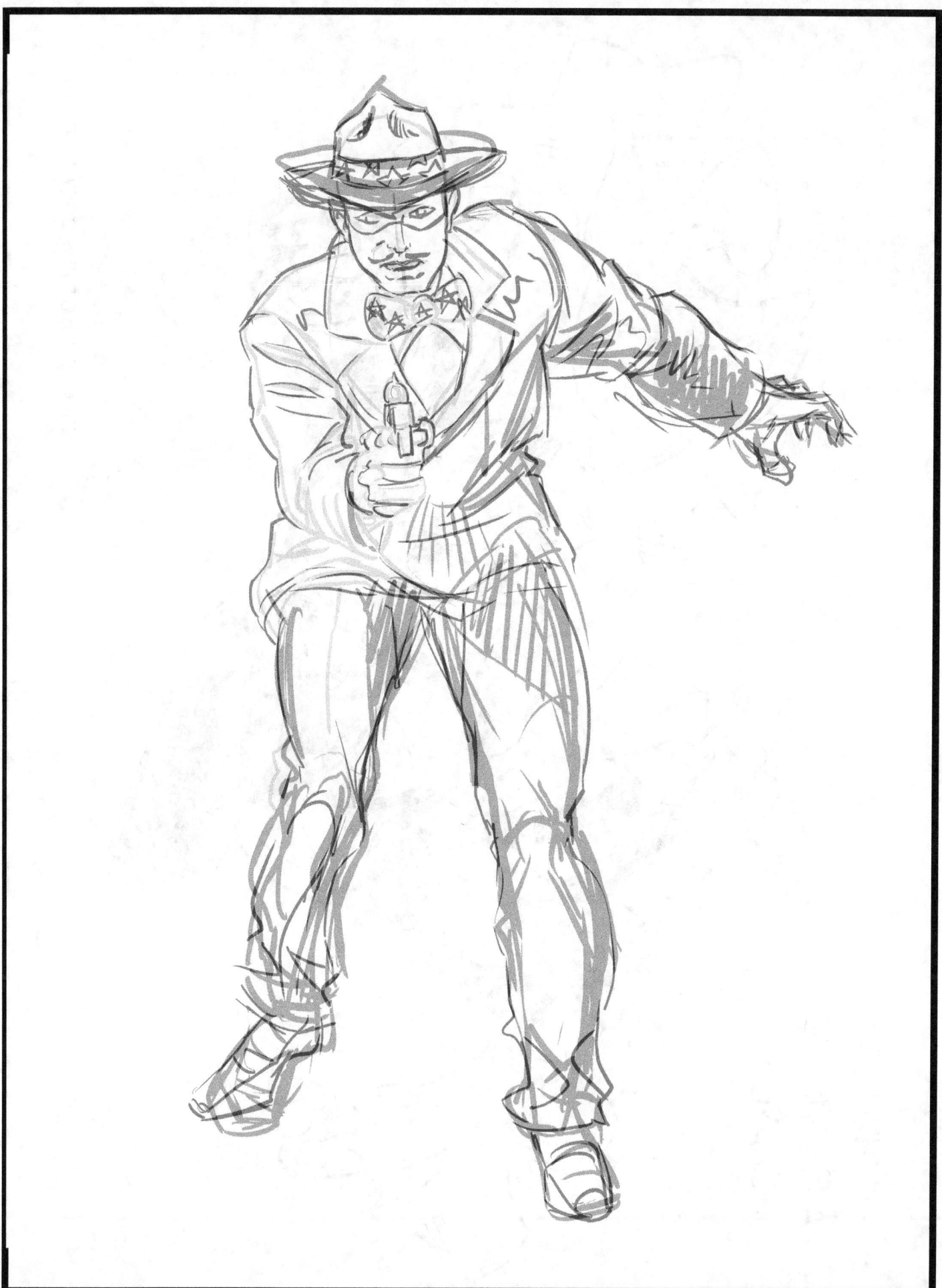

COMPLET À PARTIR DE CRAYON!

DYNAMIC MAN & DYNAMIC BOY – CHESLER

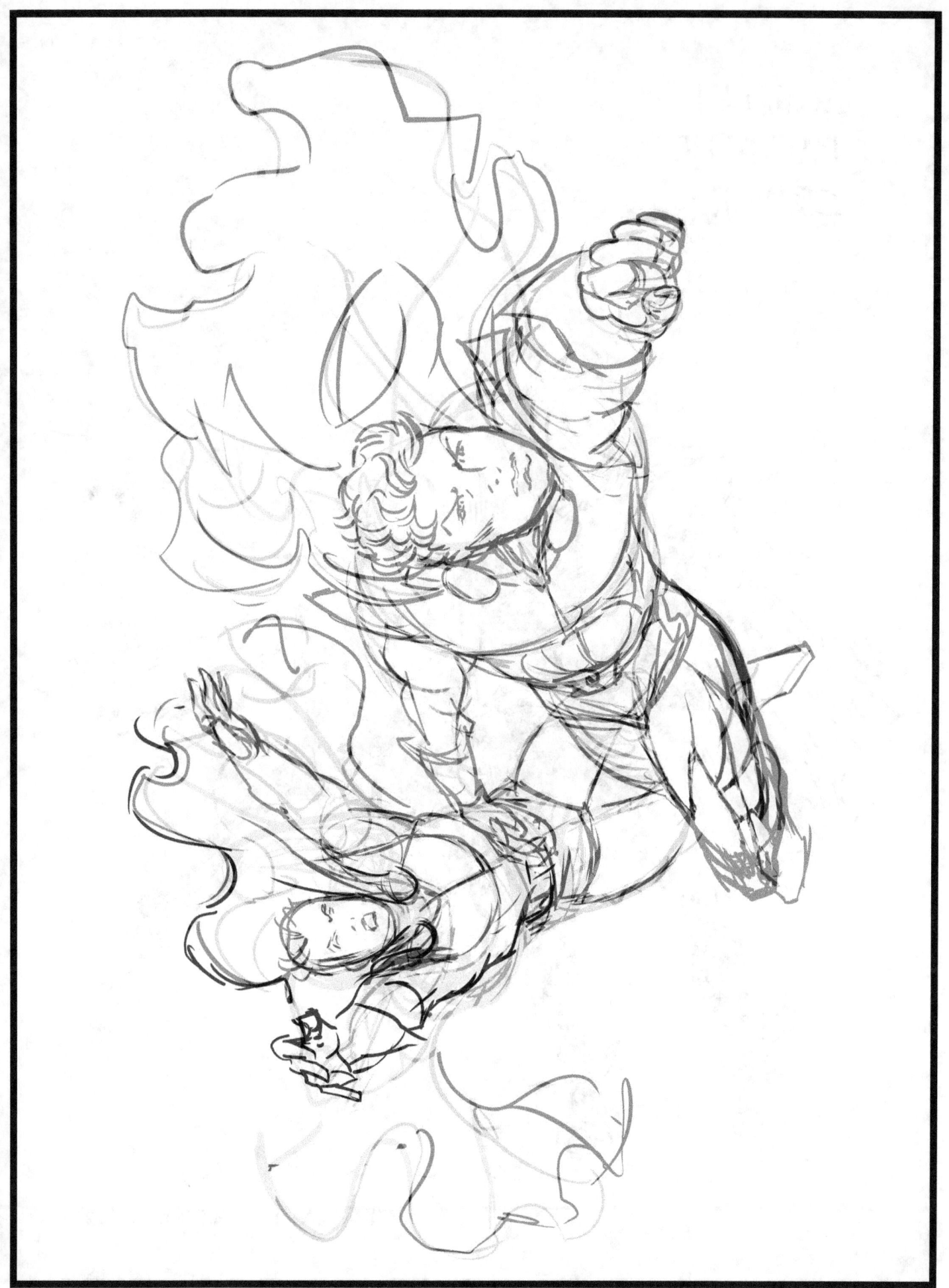

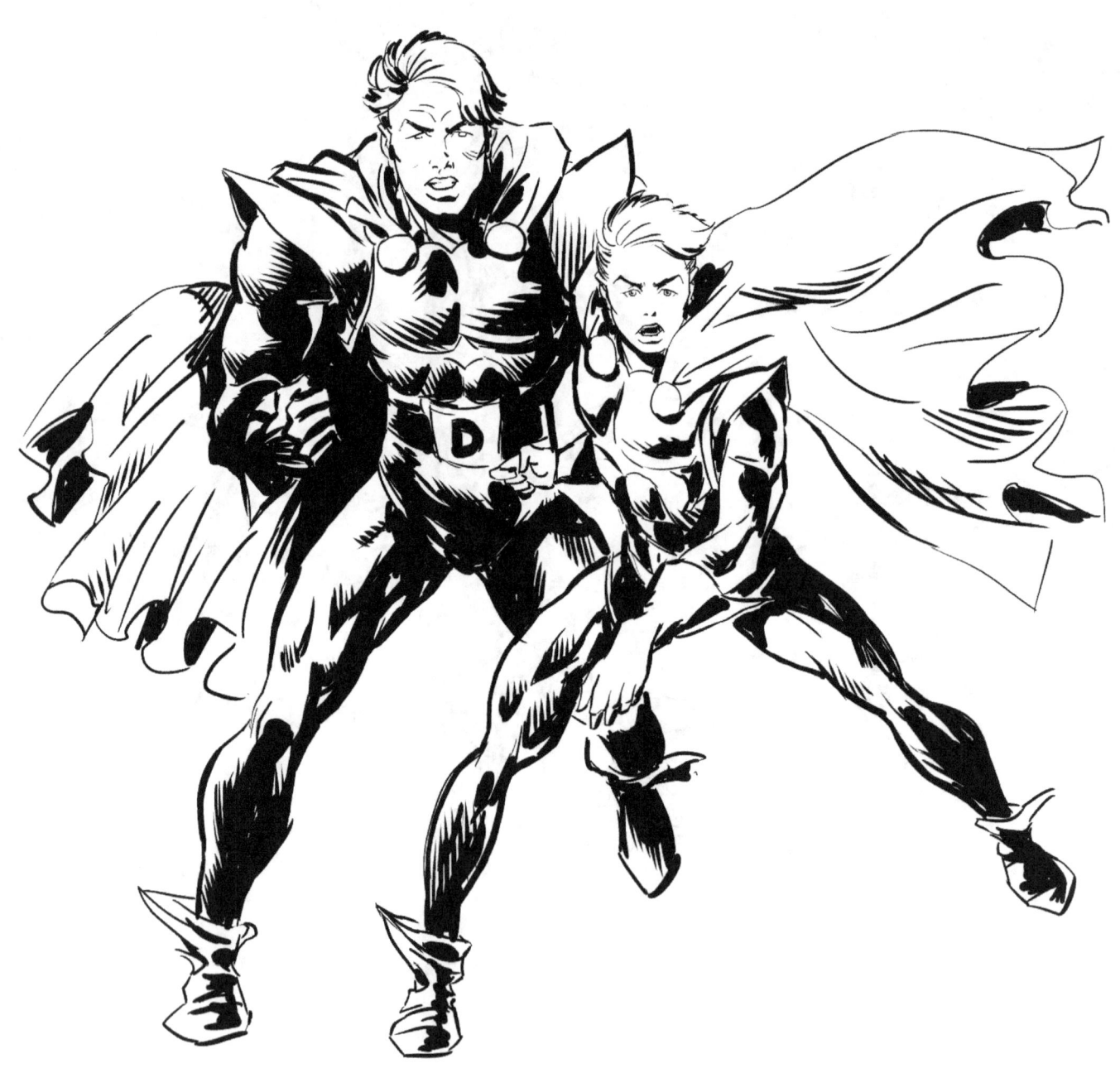

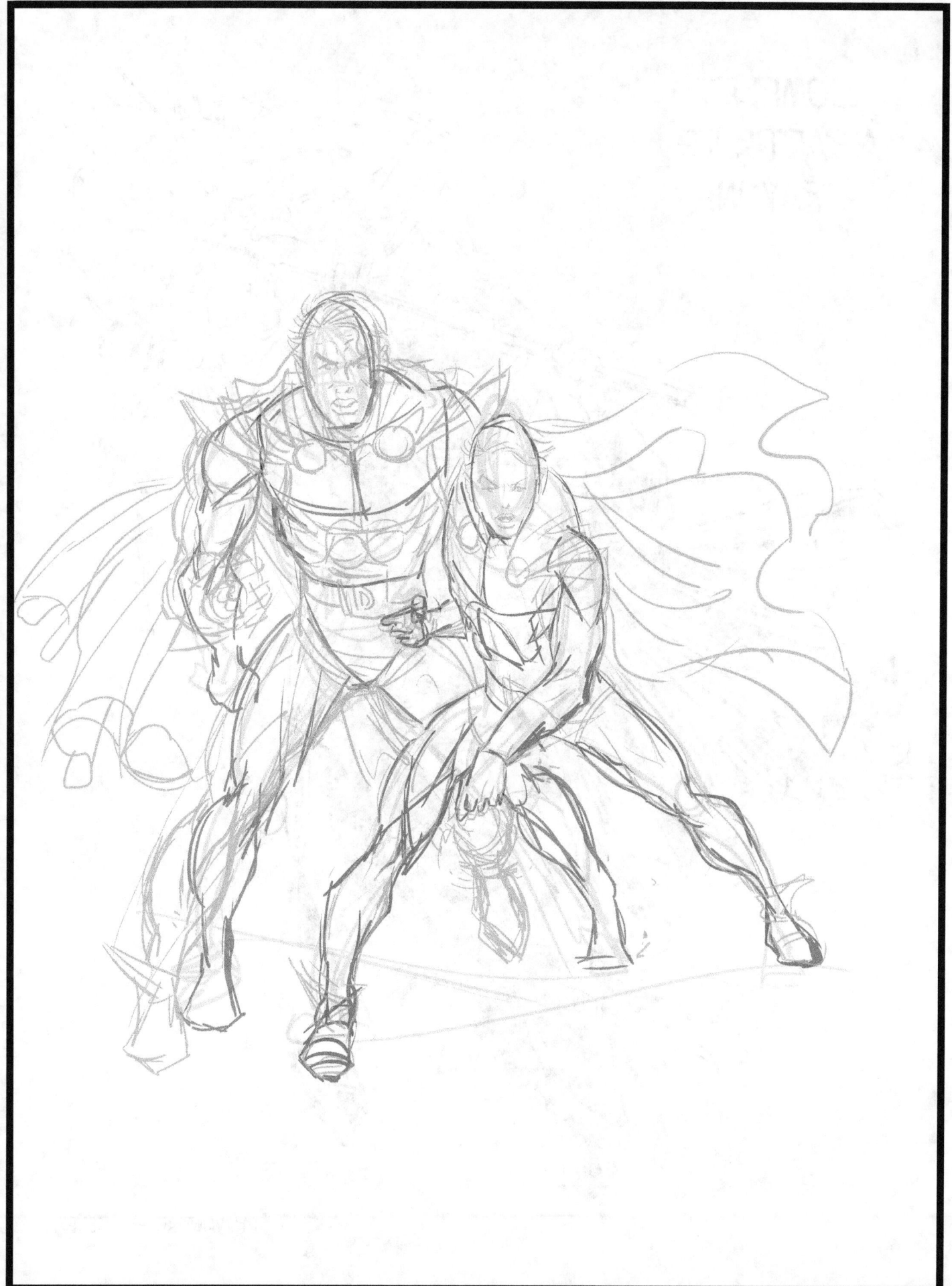

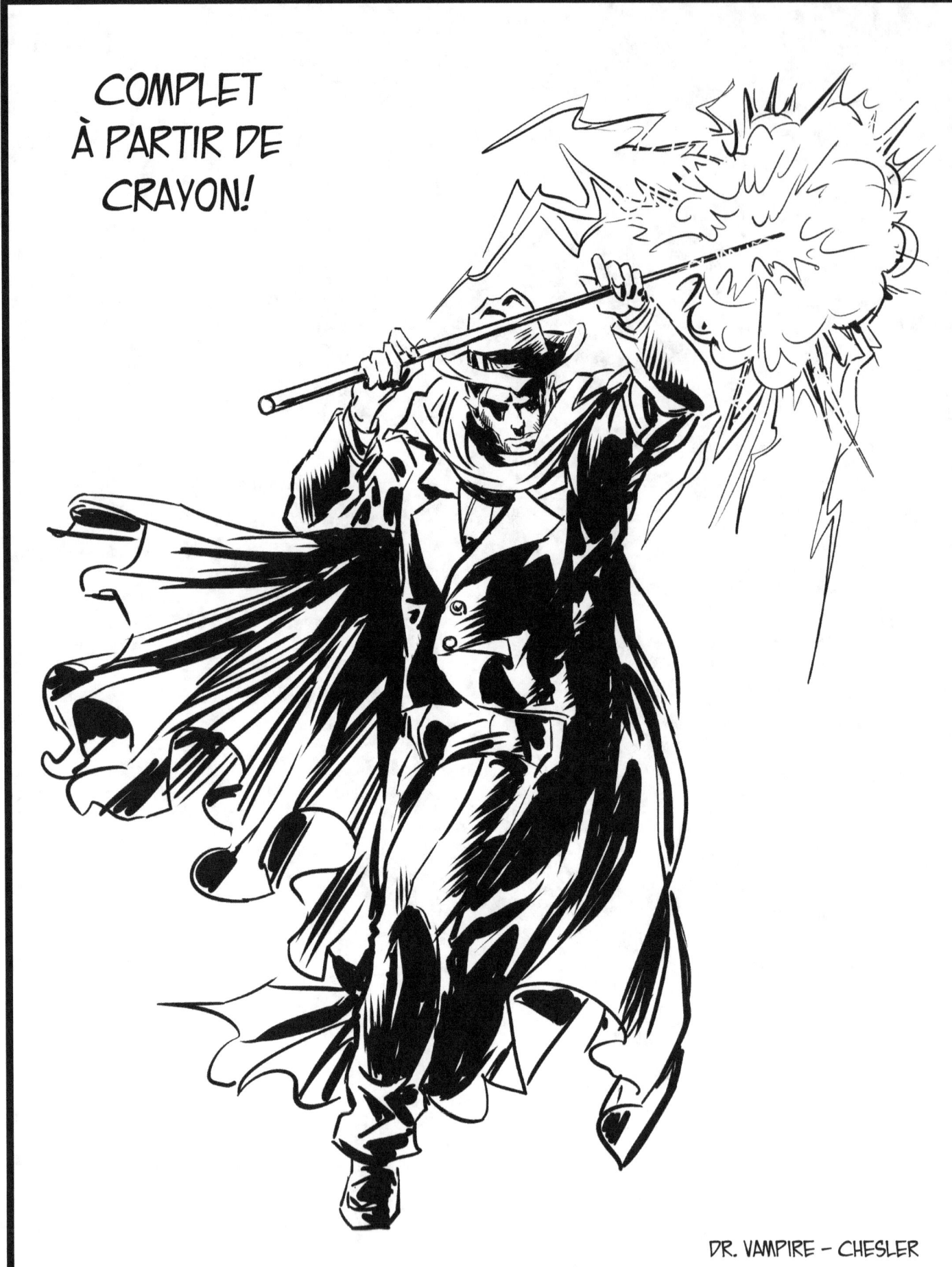

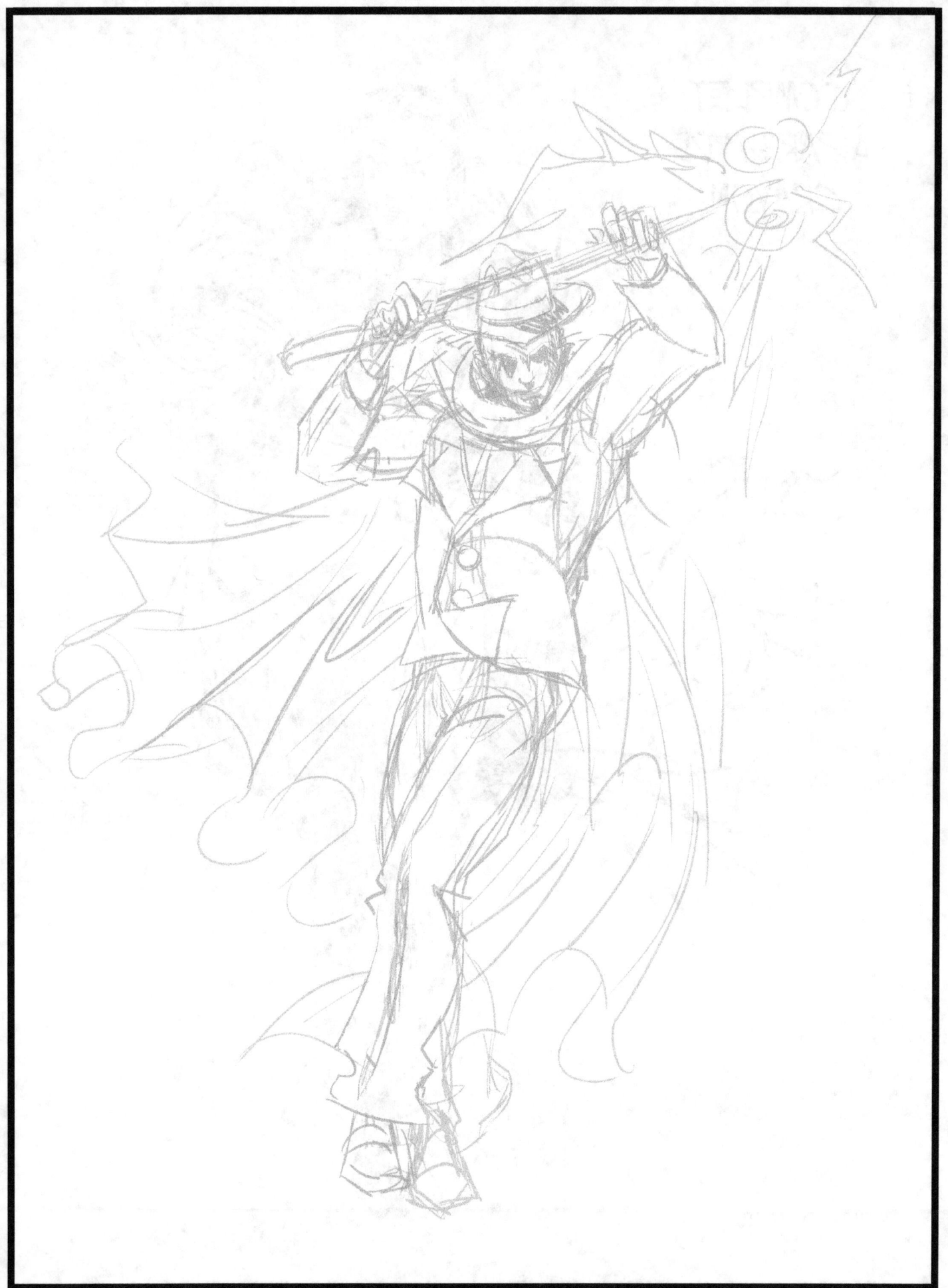

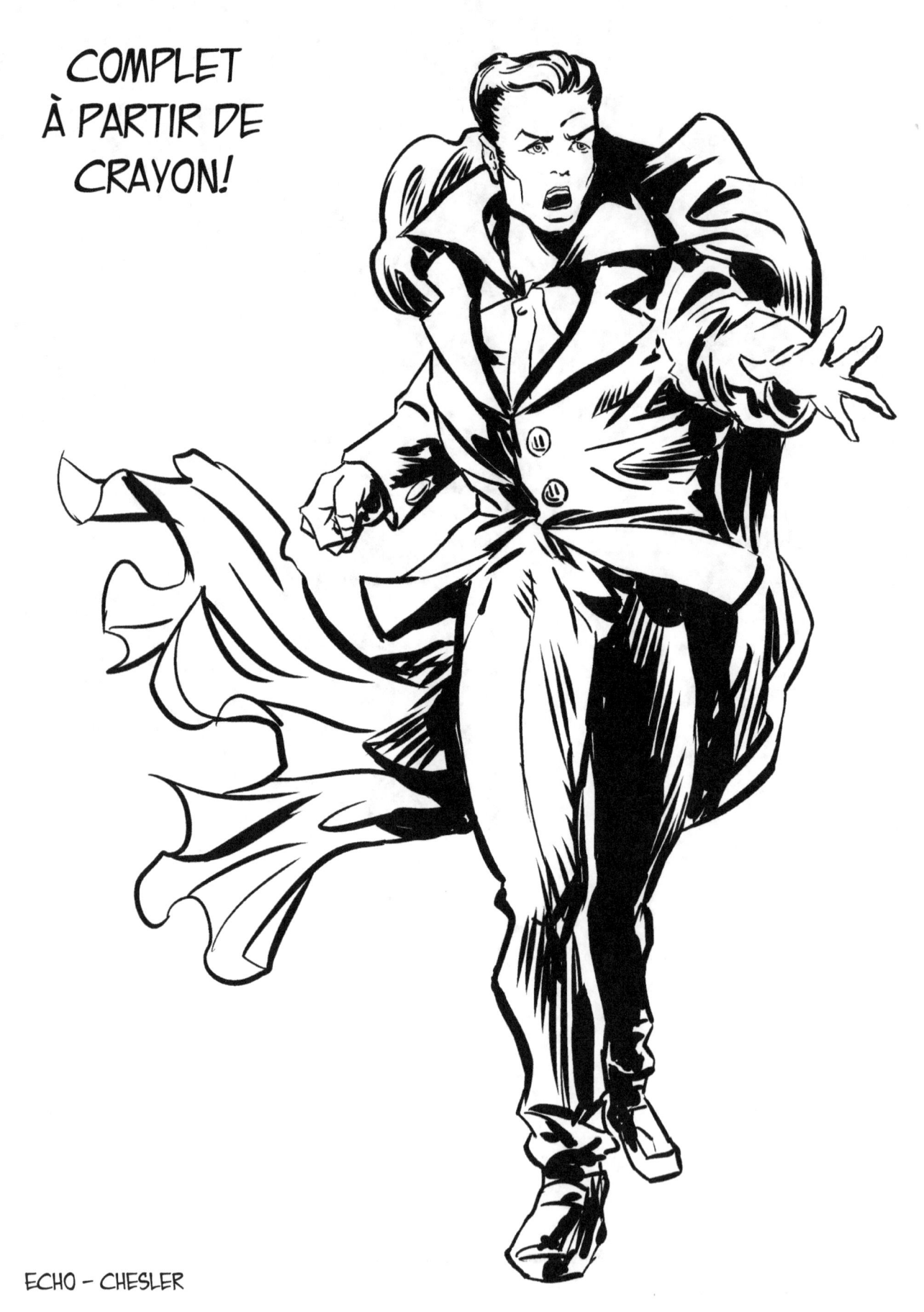

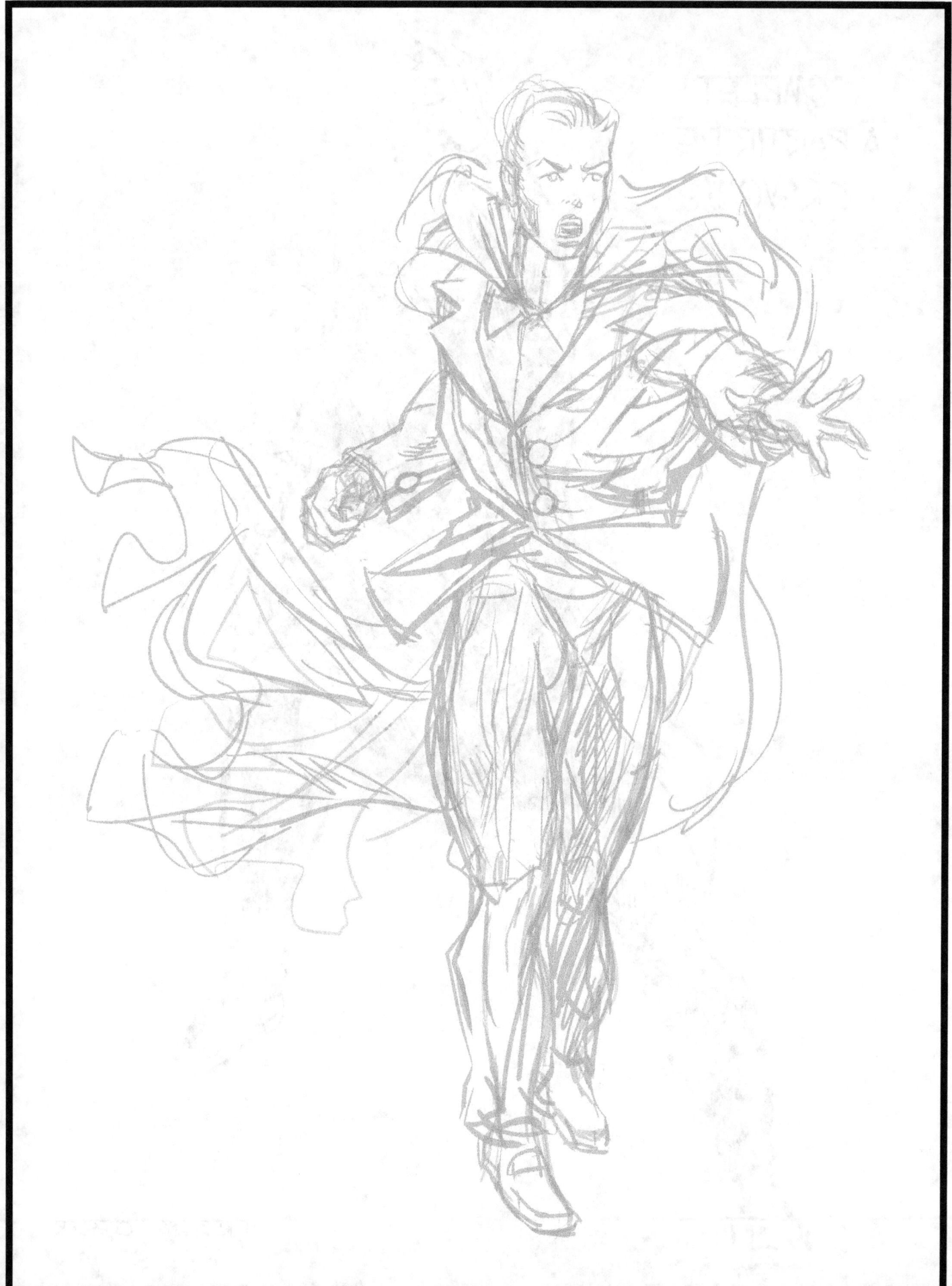

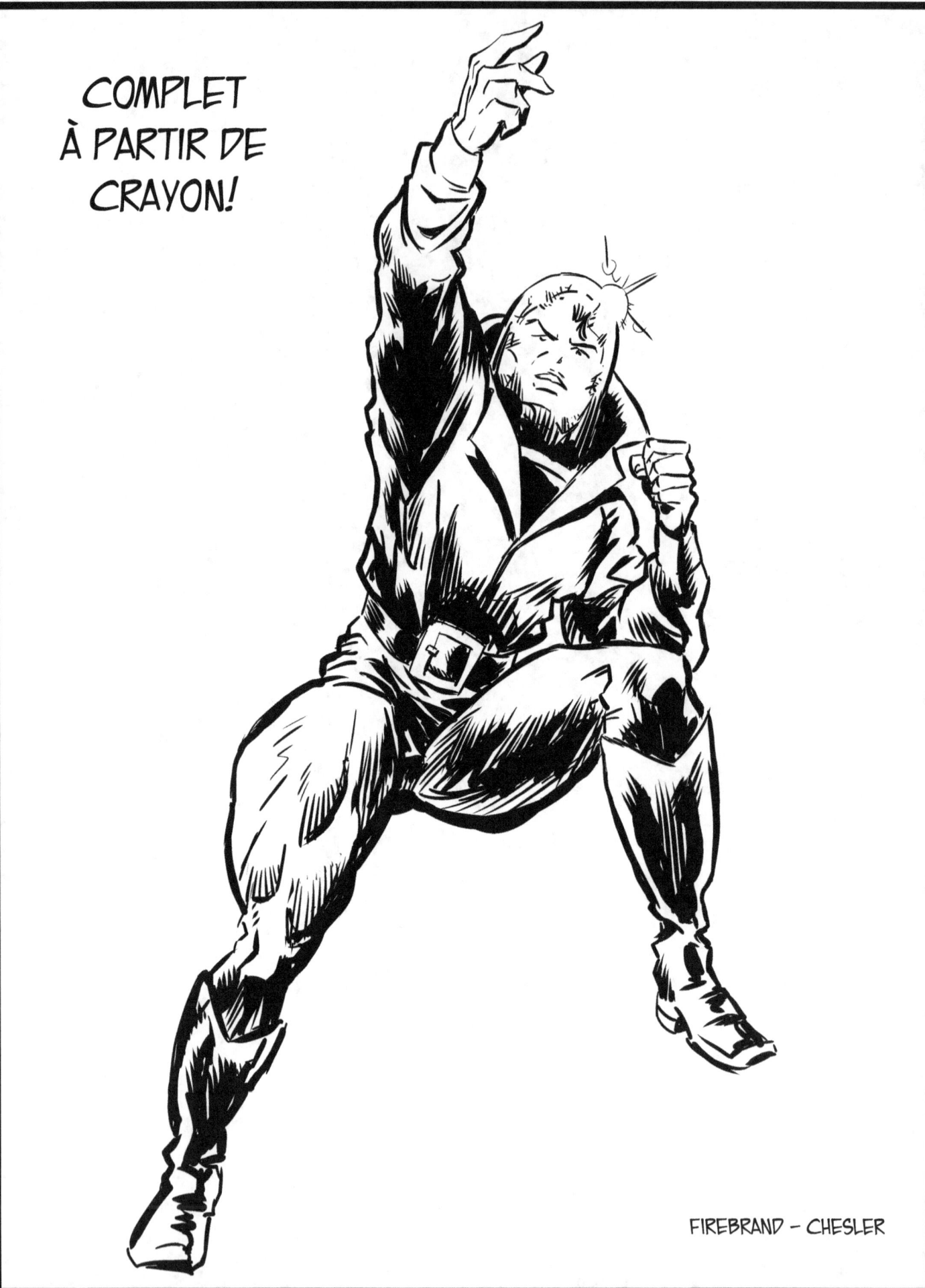

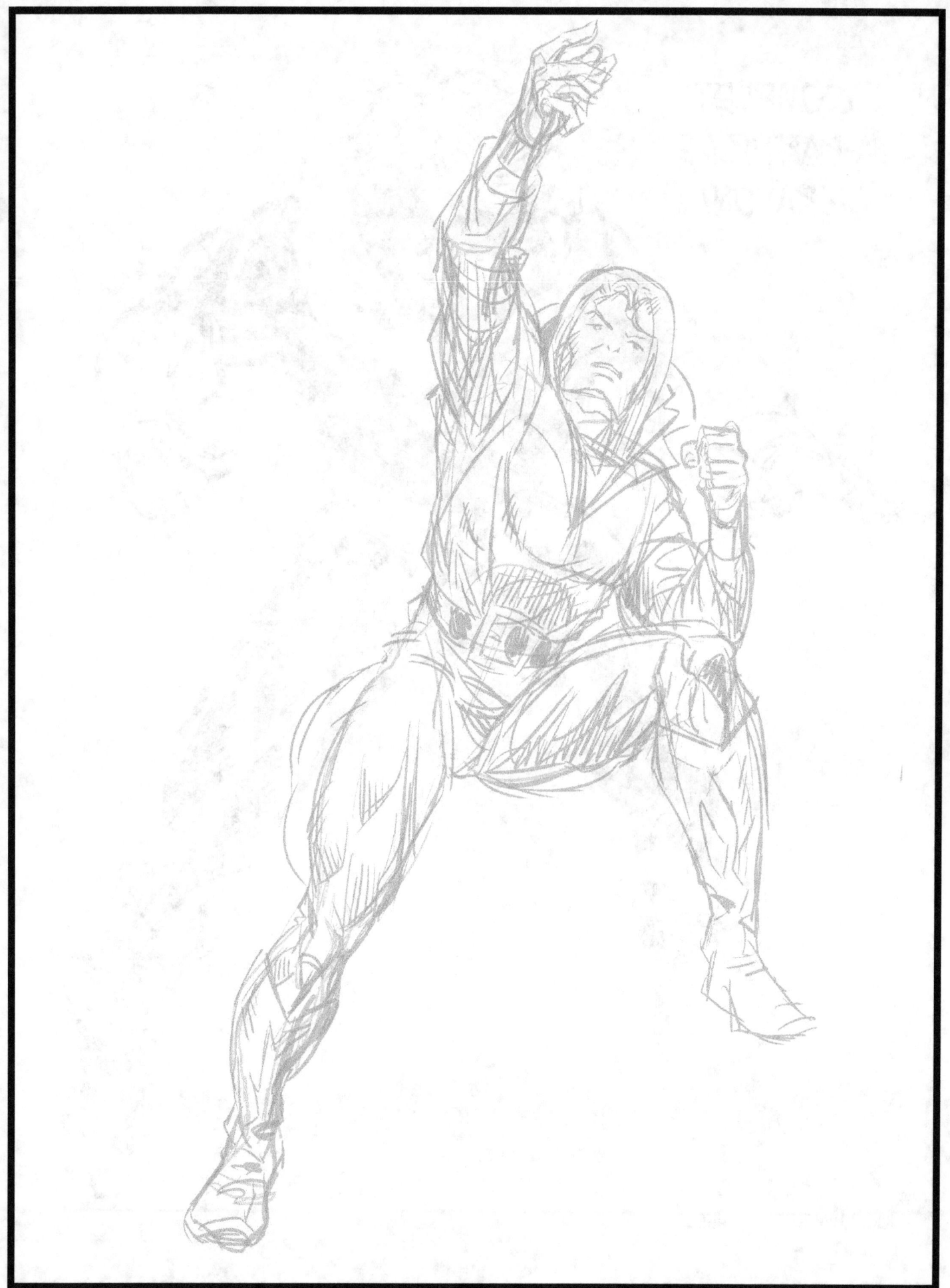

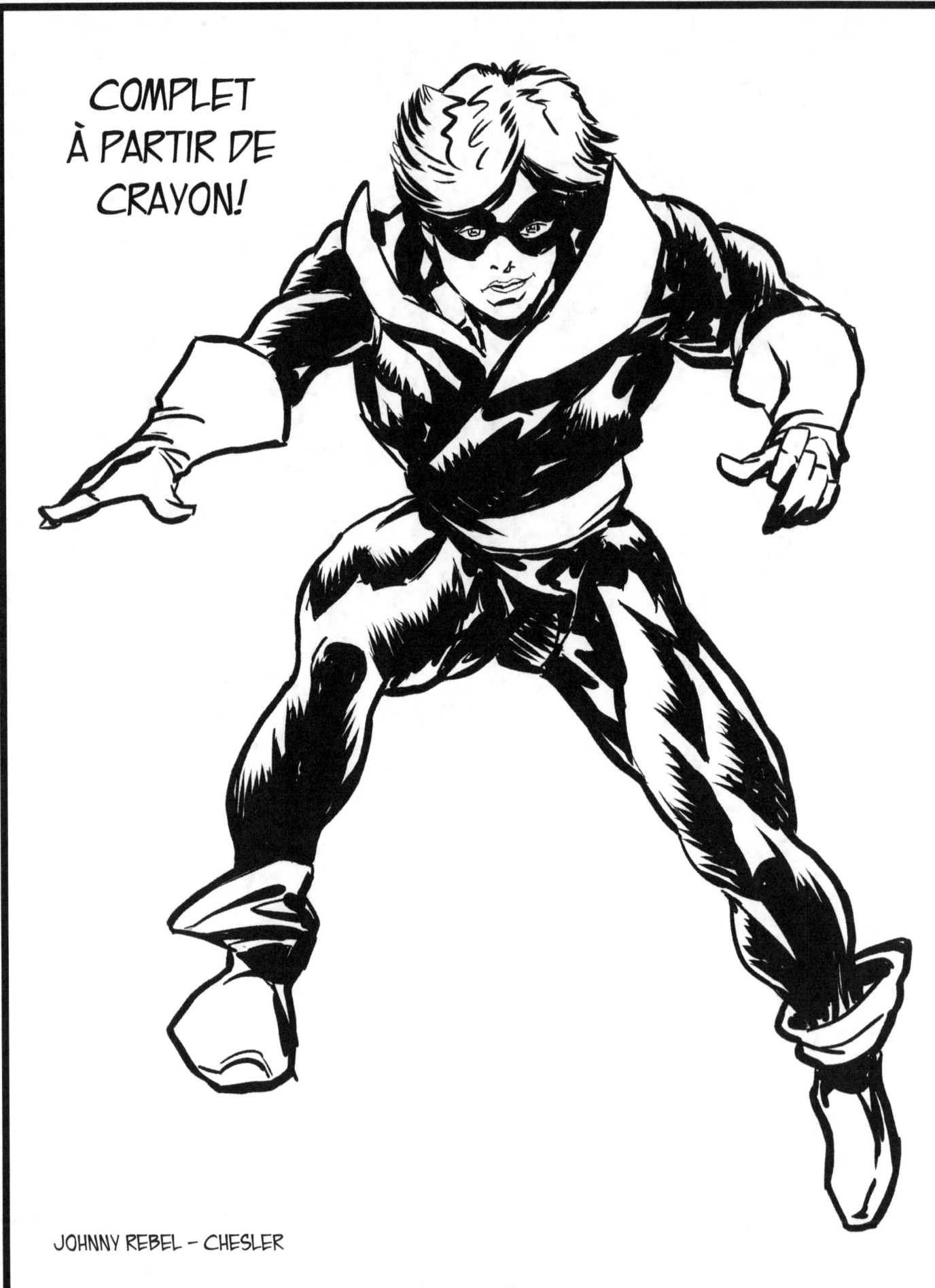

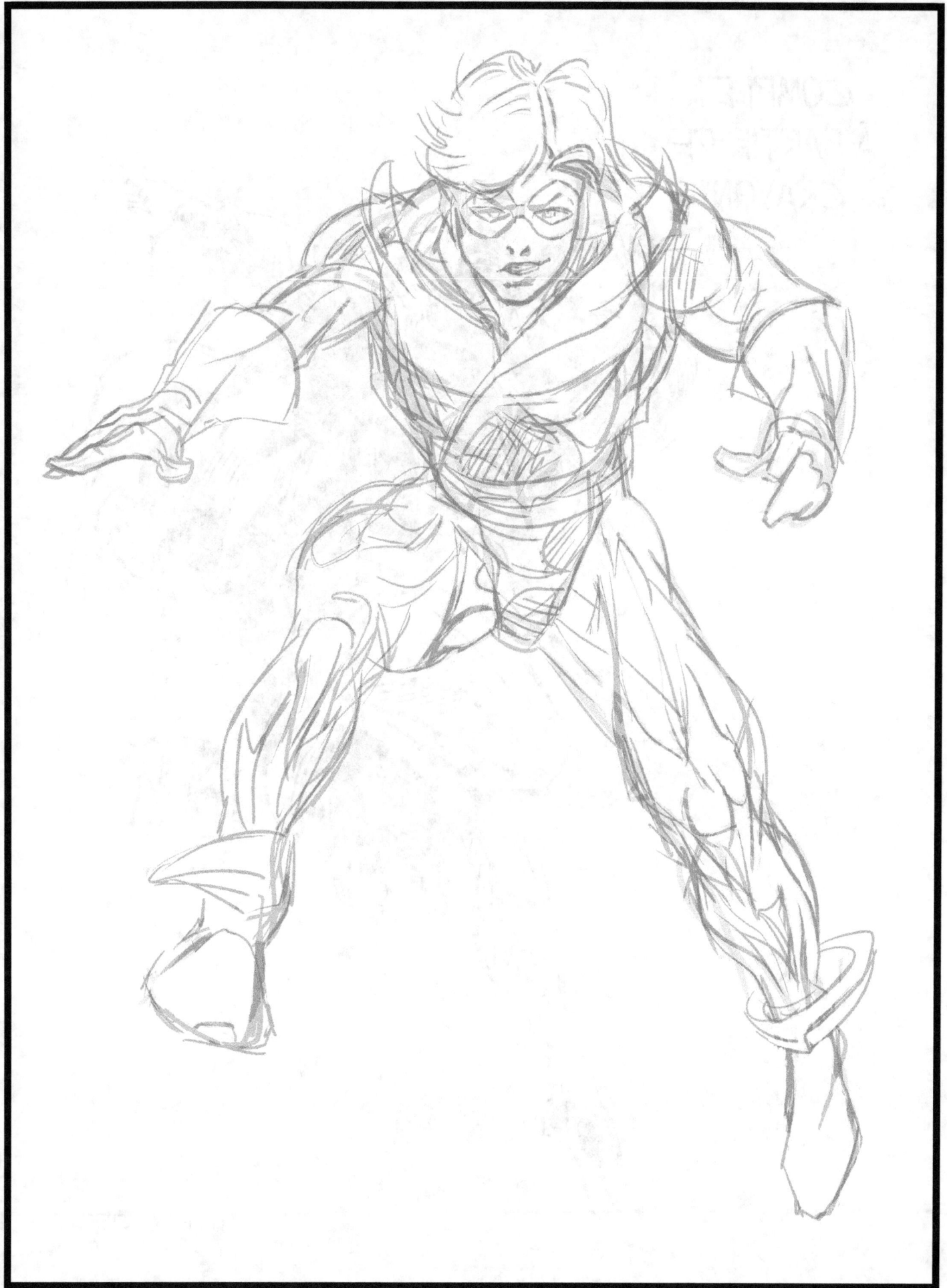

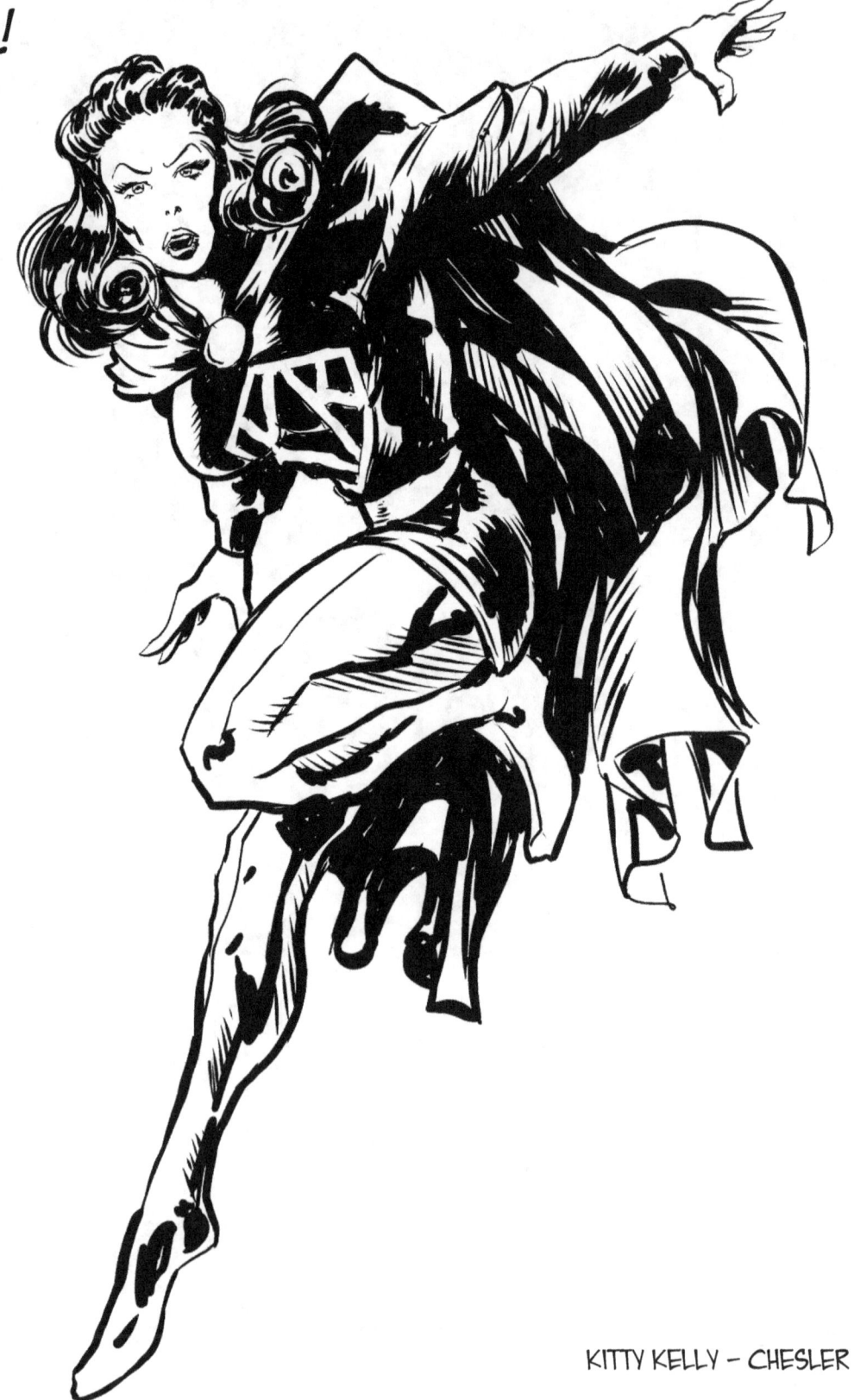

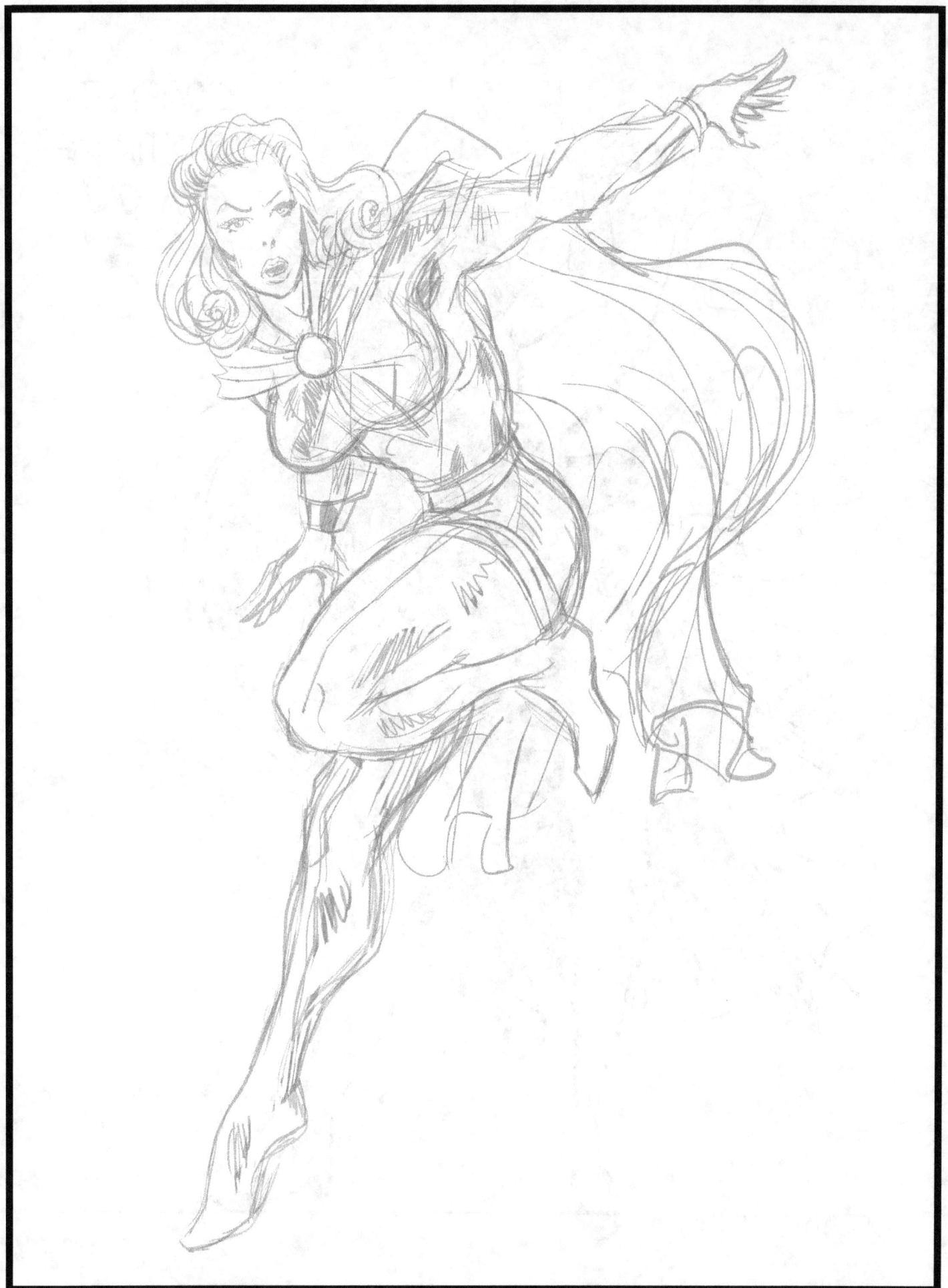

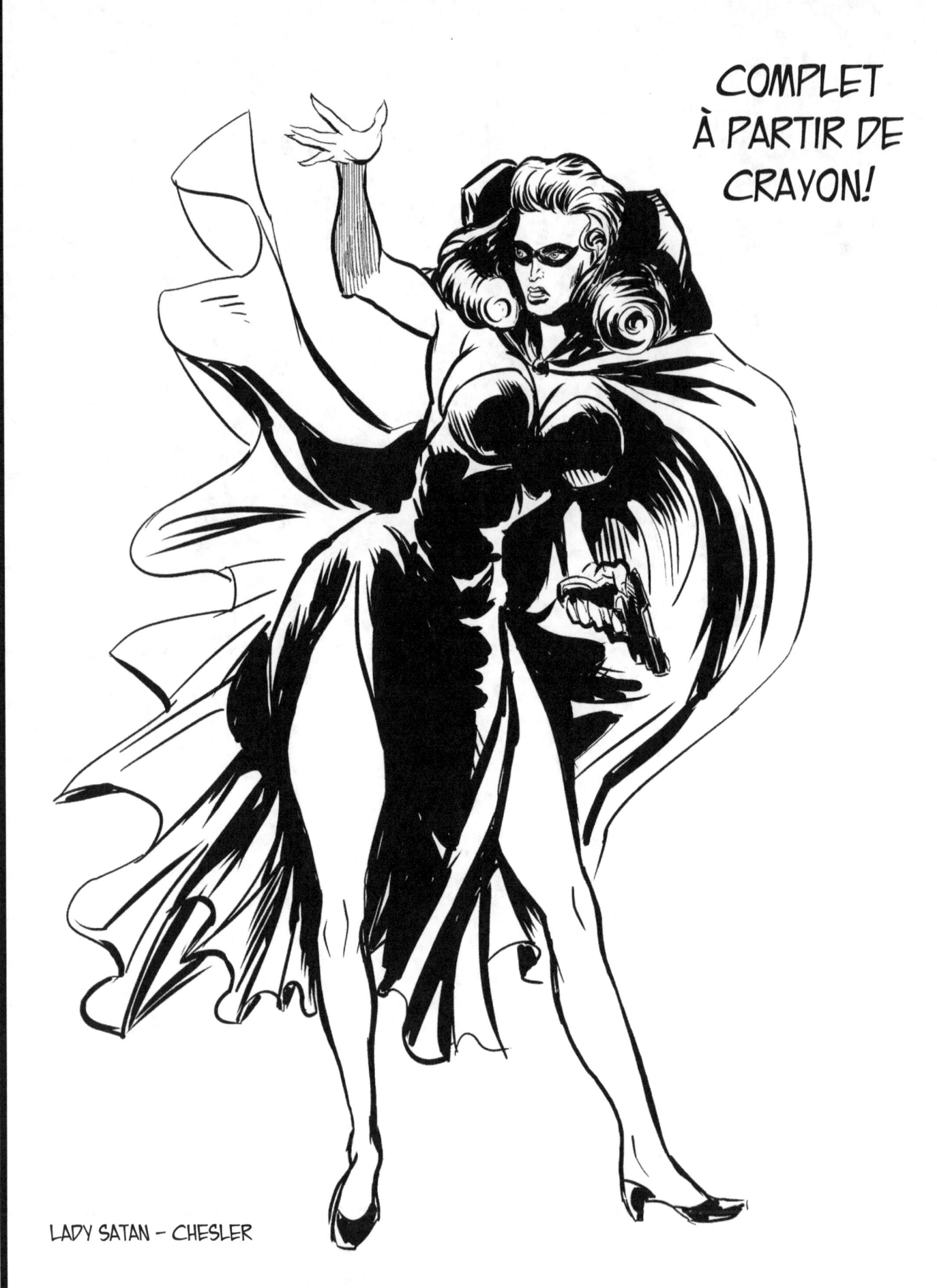

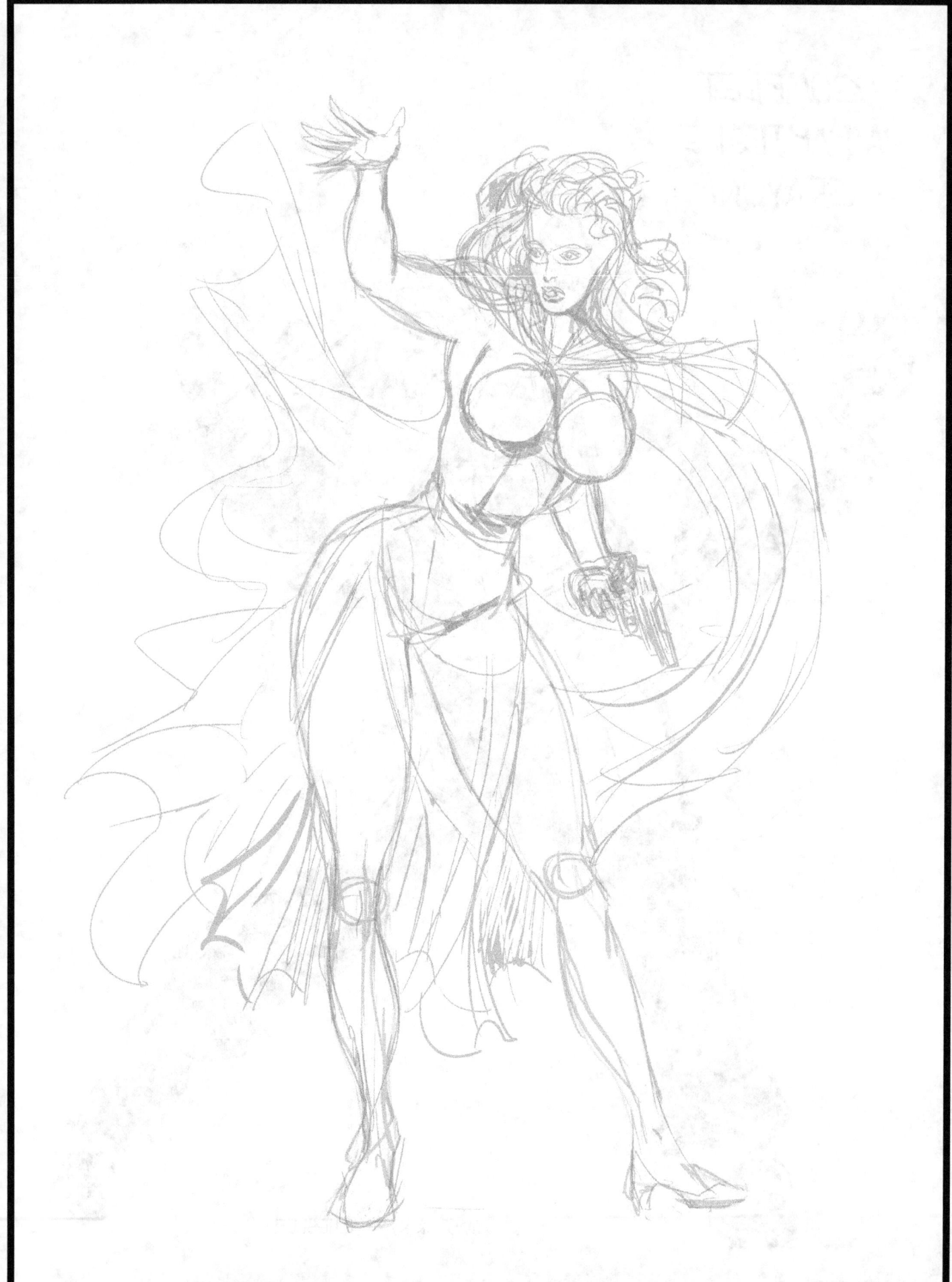

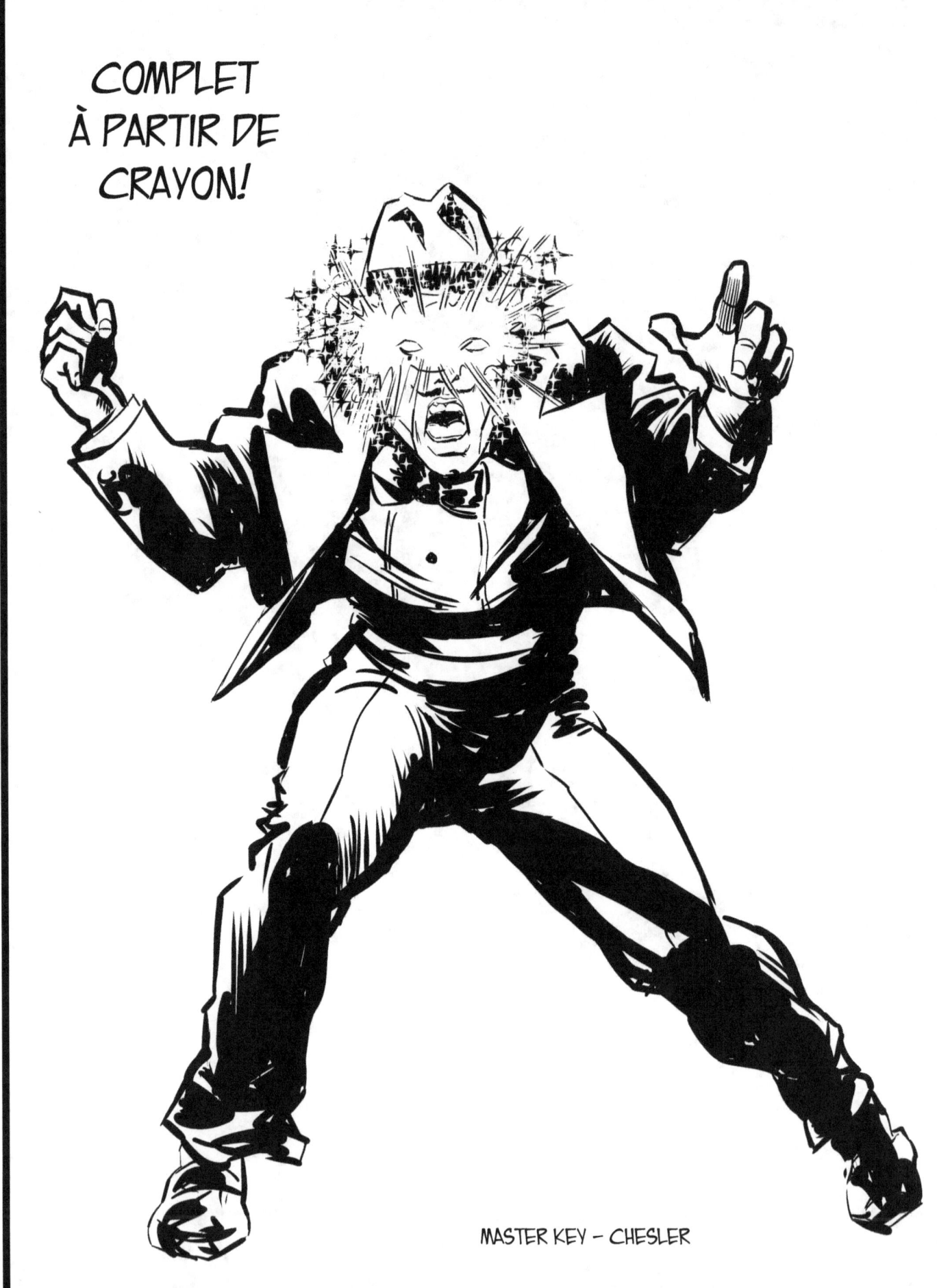

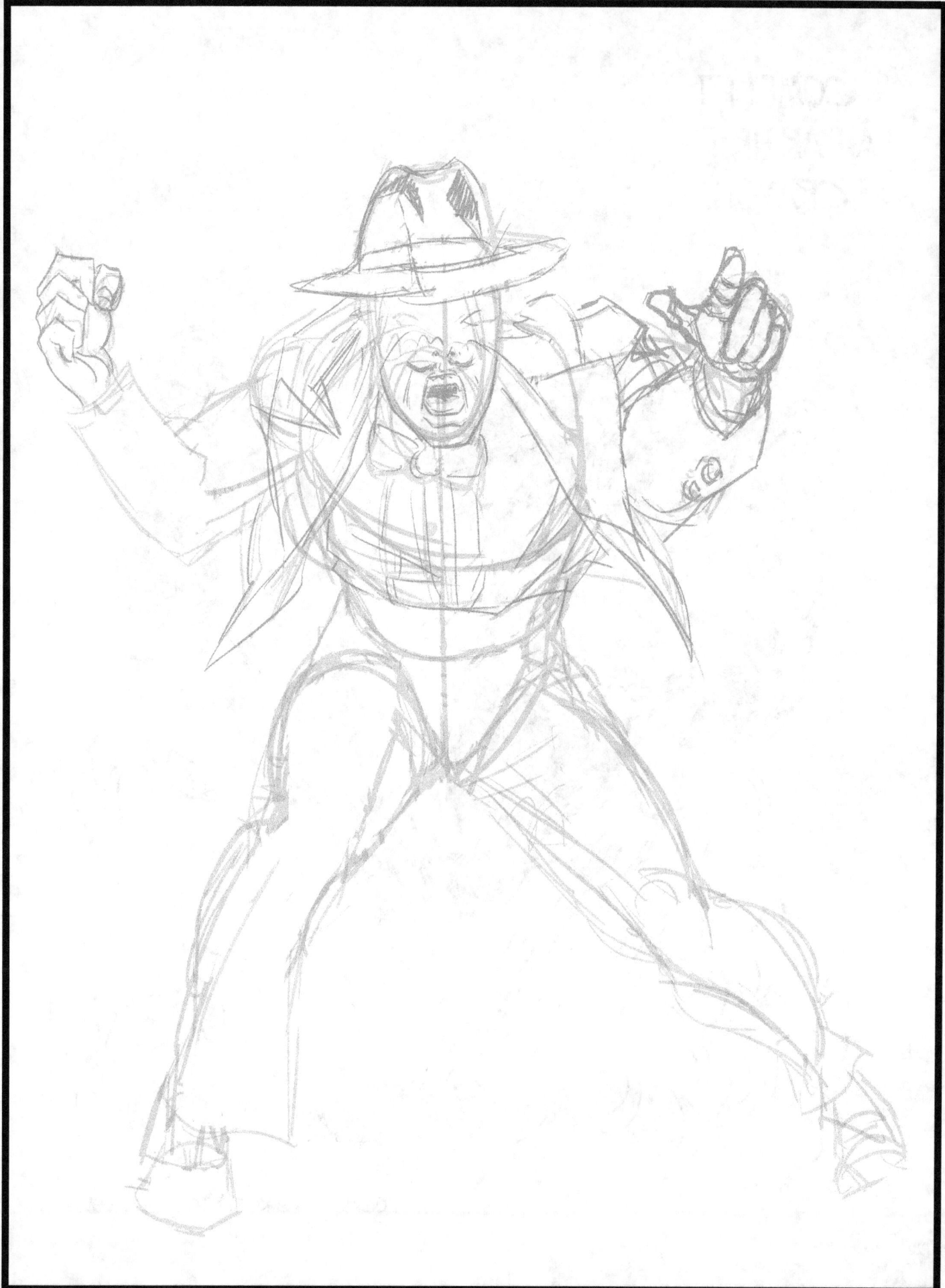

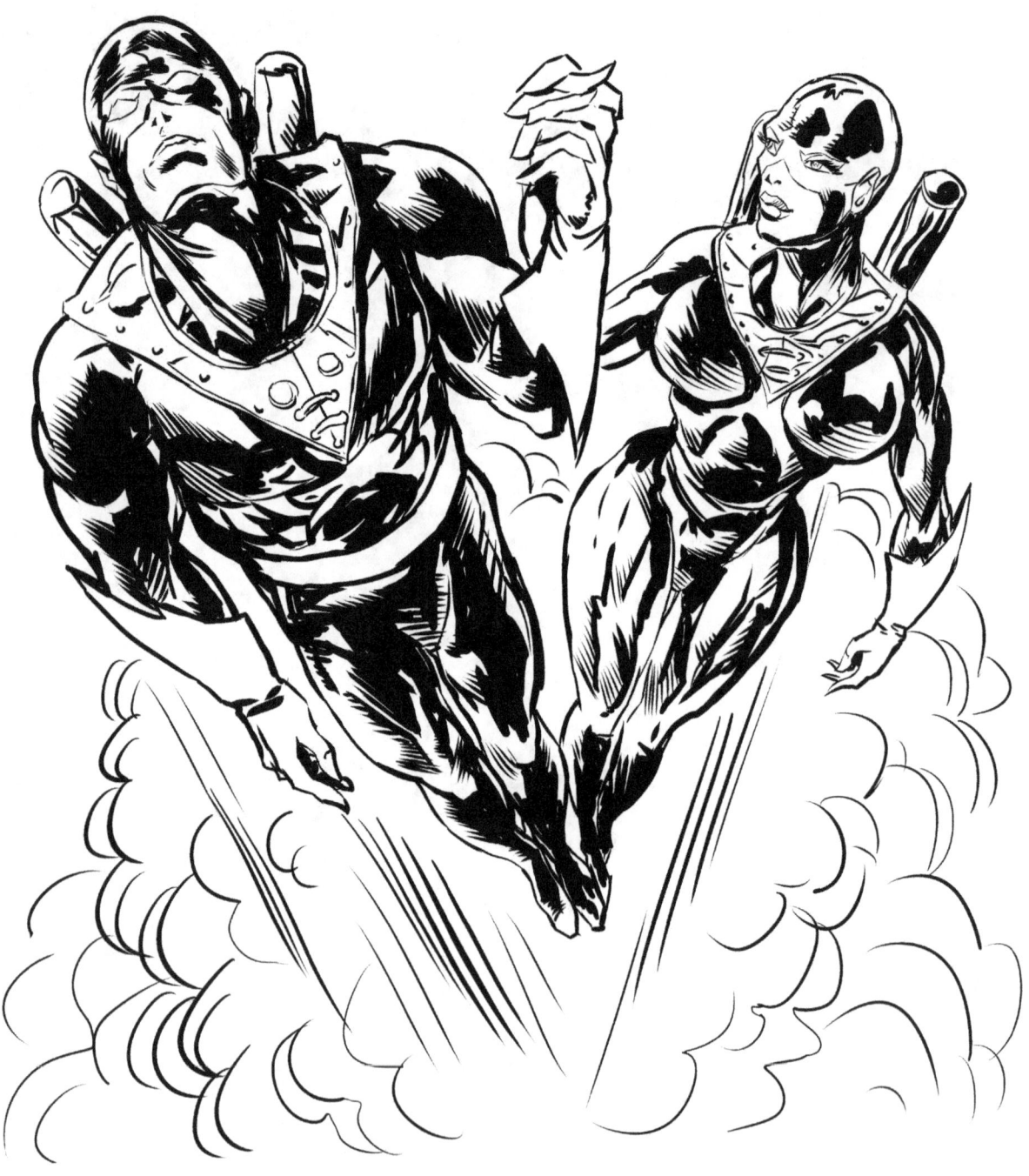

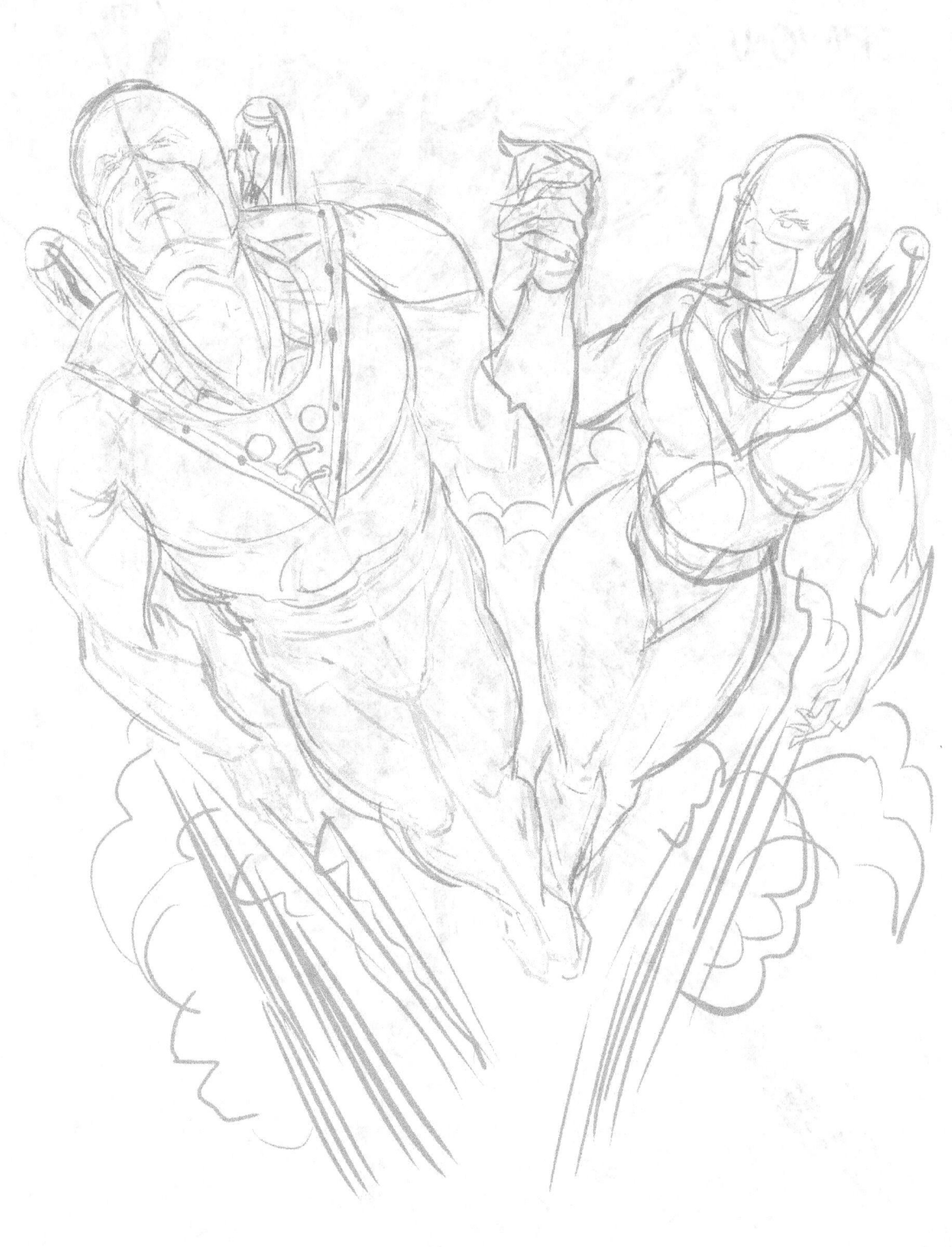

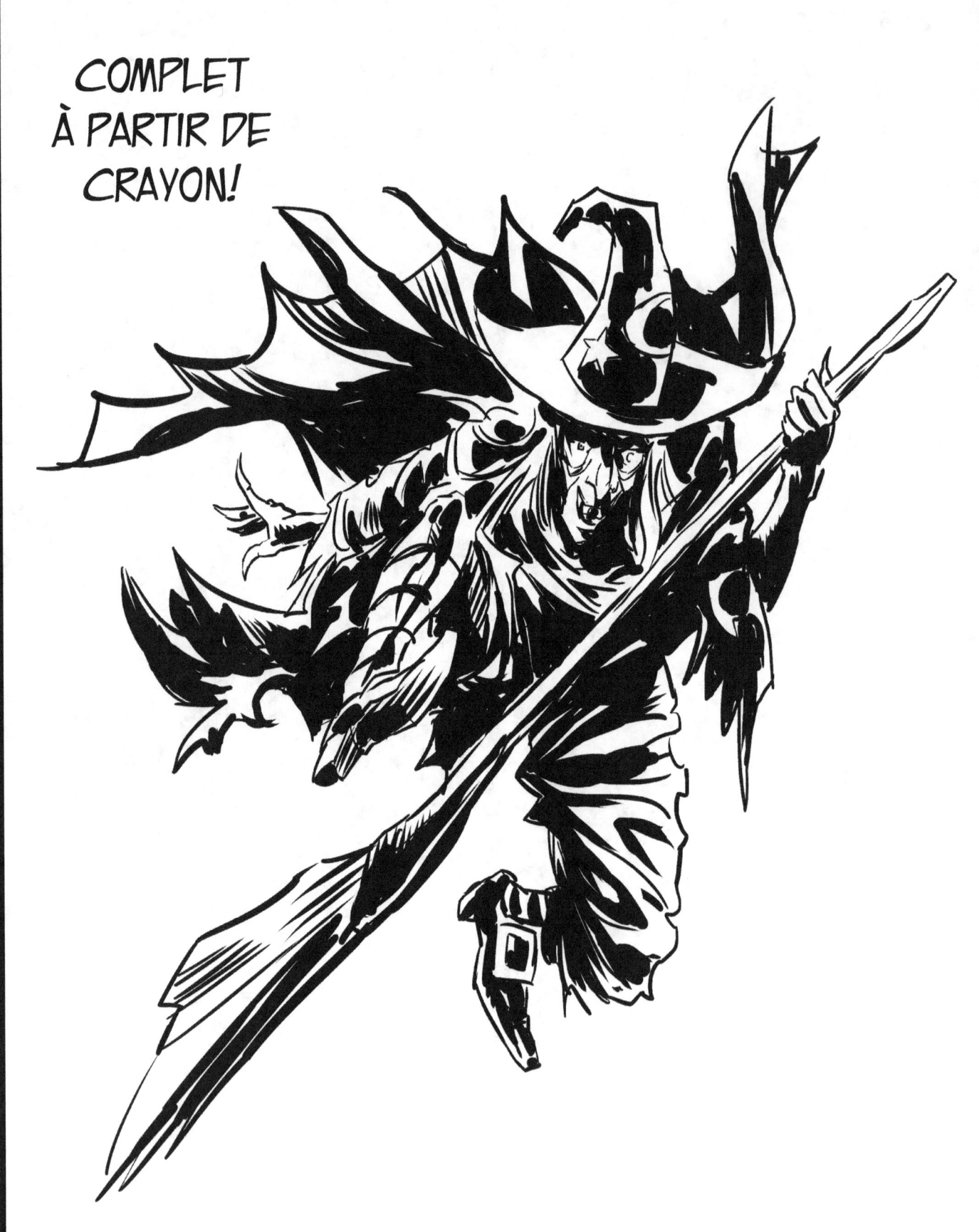

COMPLET À PARTIR DE CRAYON!

MOTHER HUBBARD – CHESLER

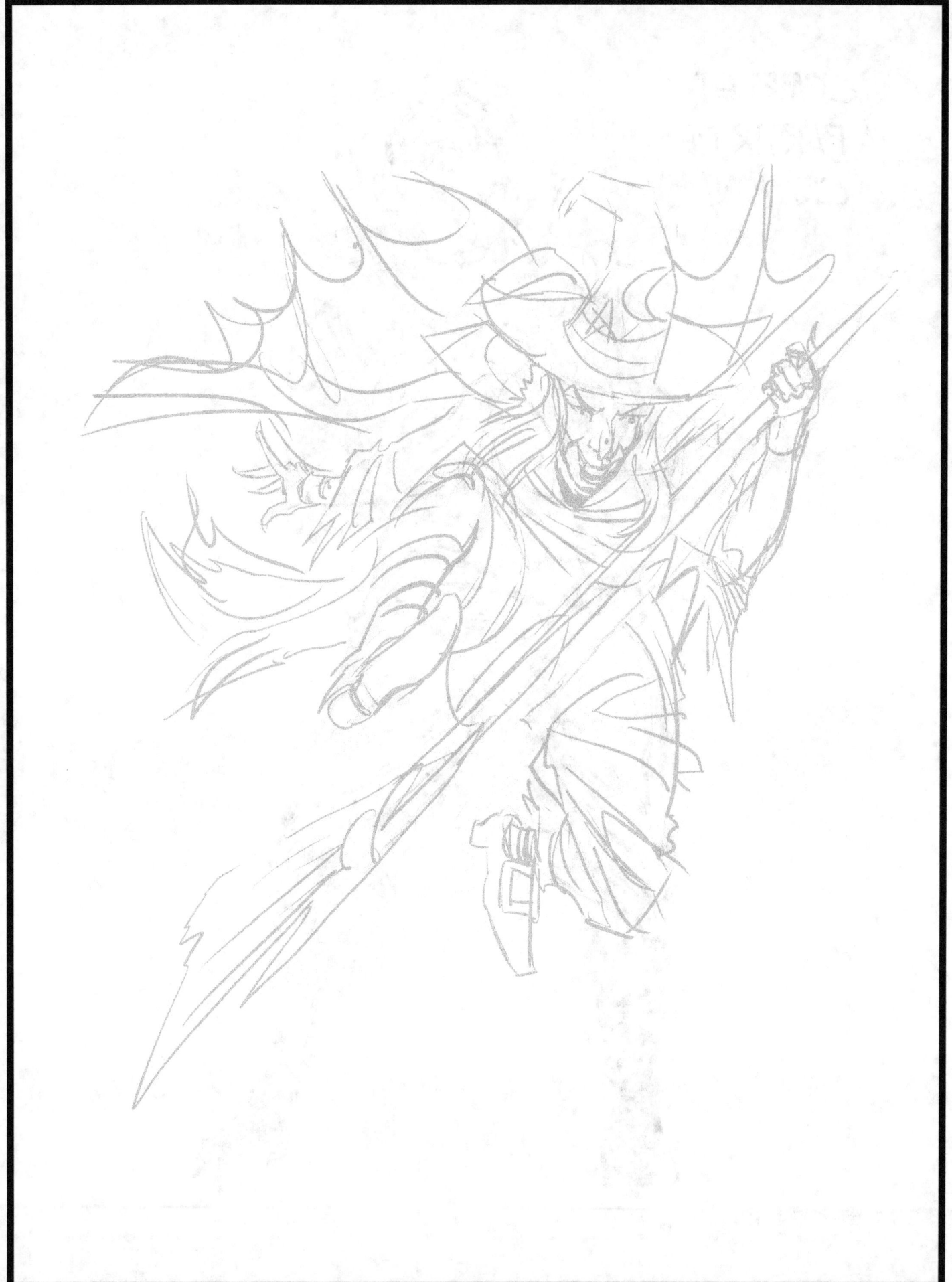

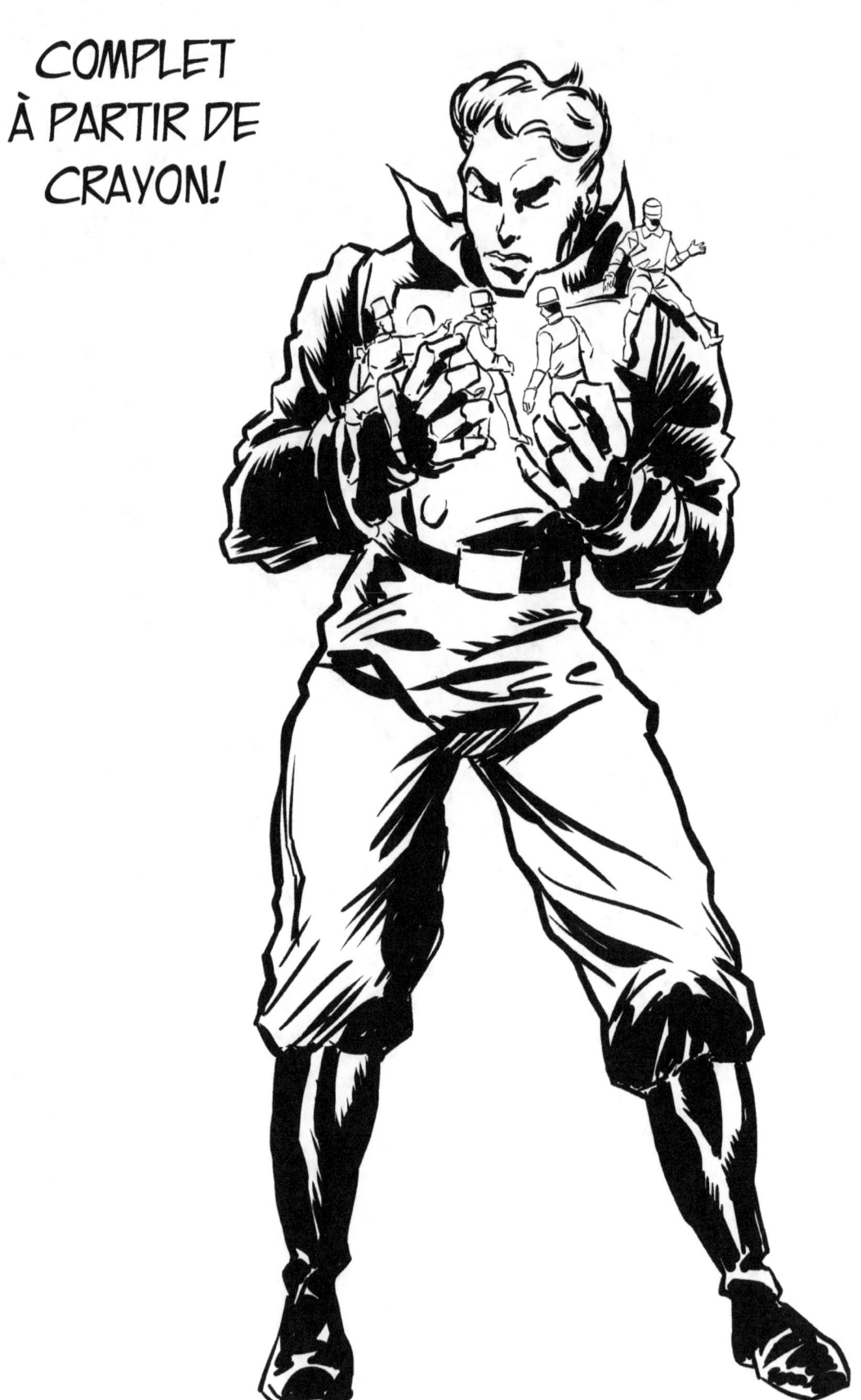

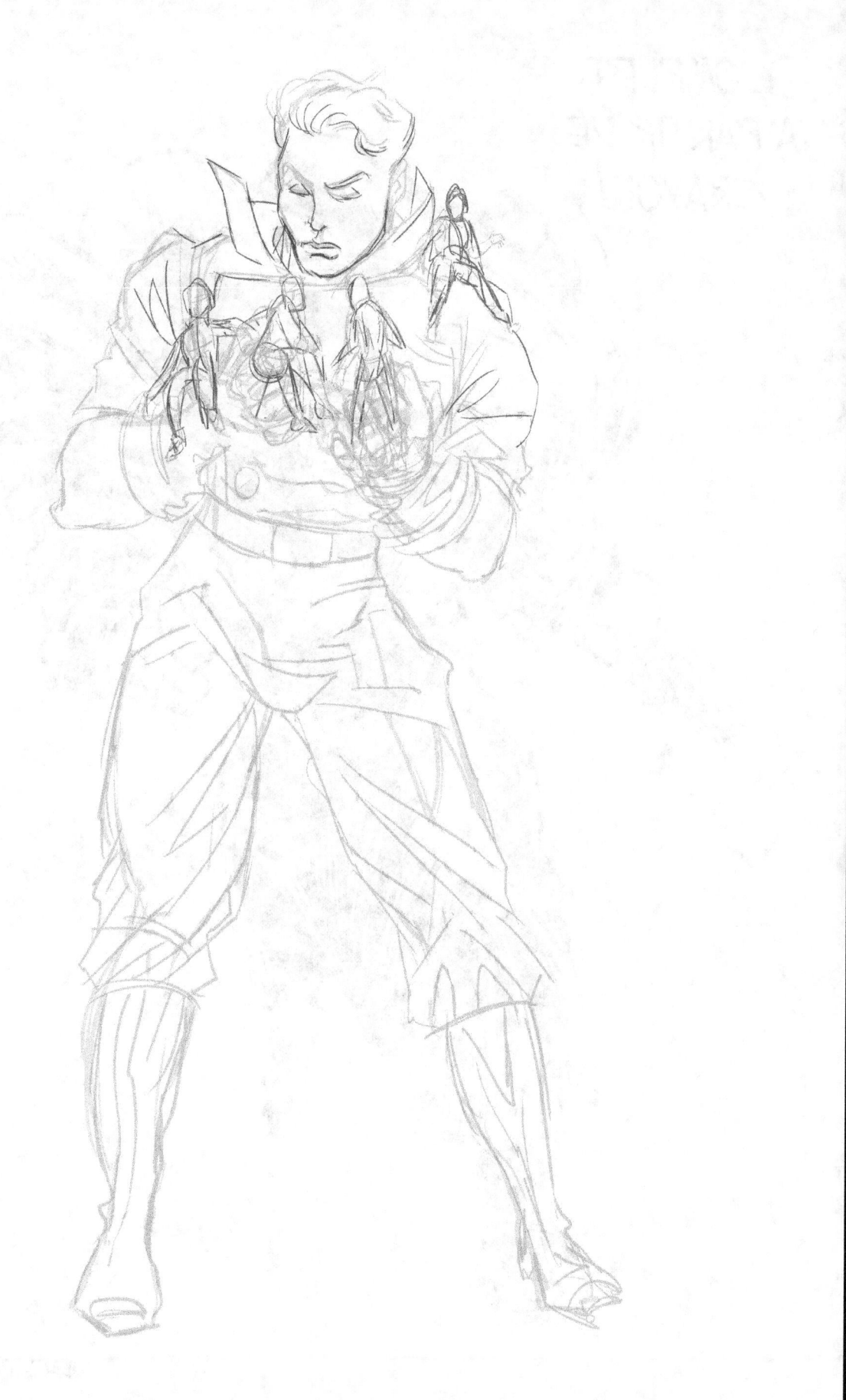

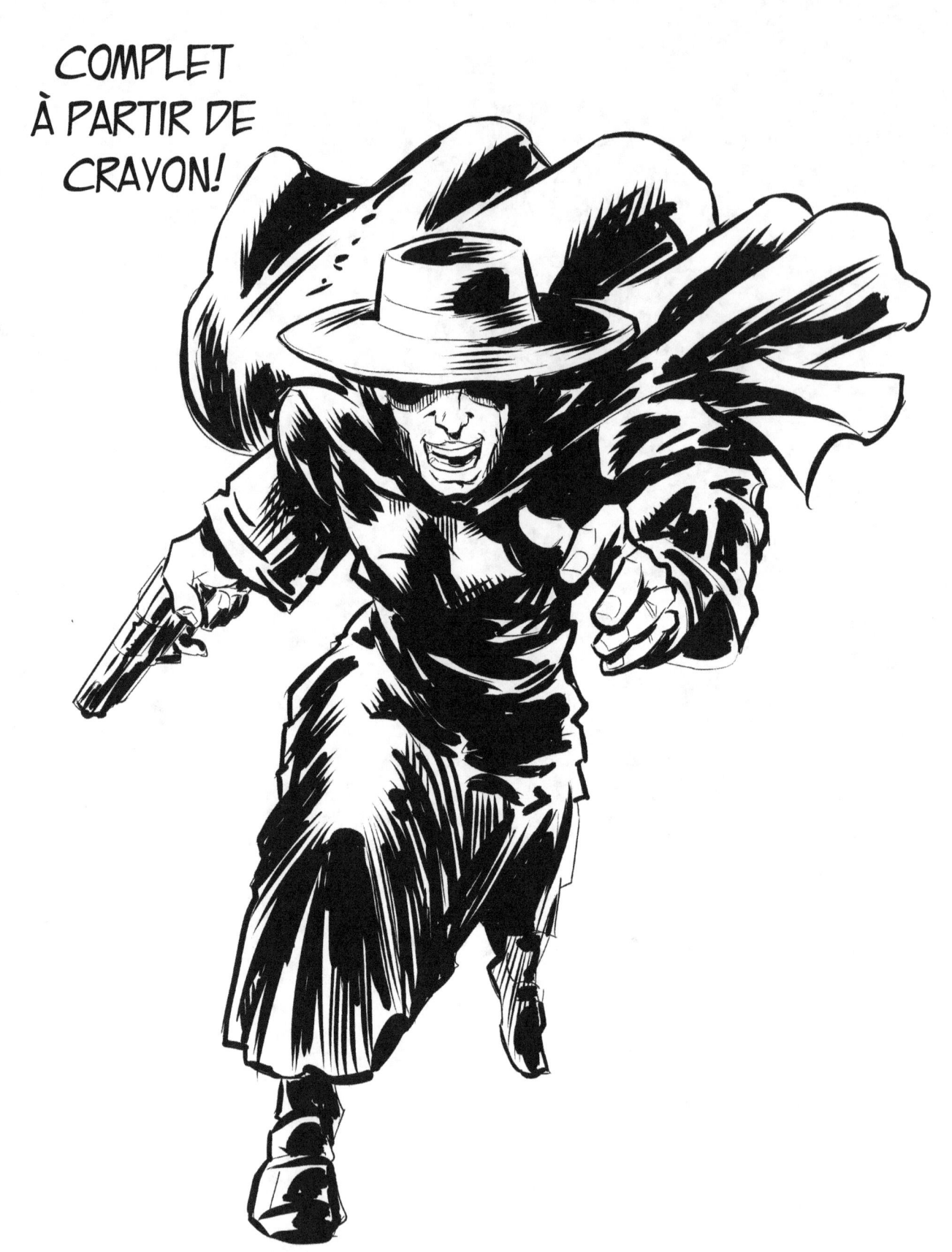

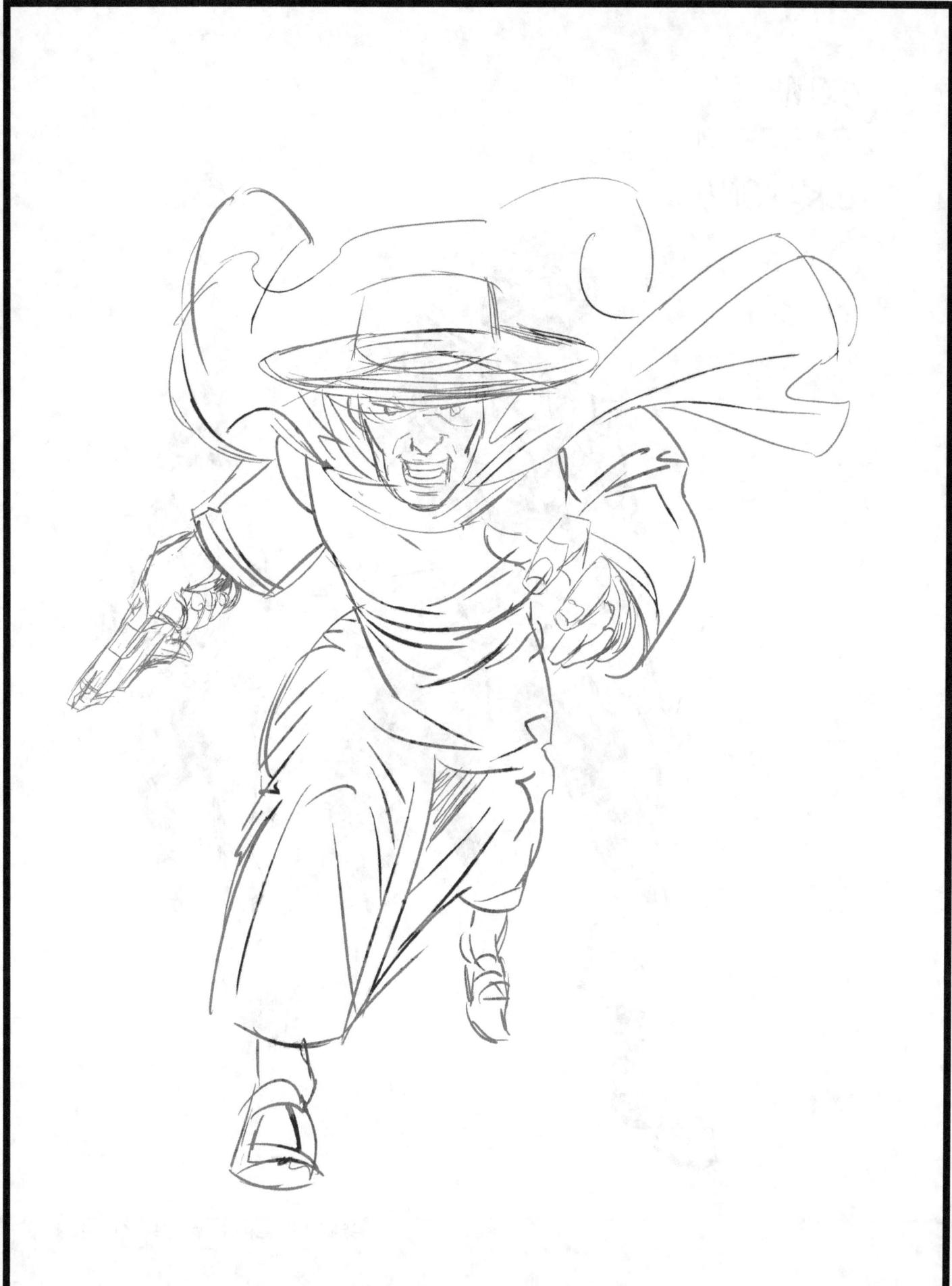

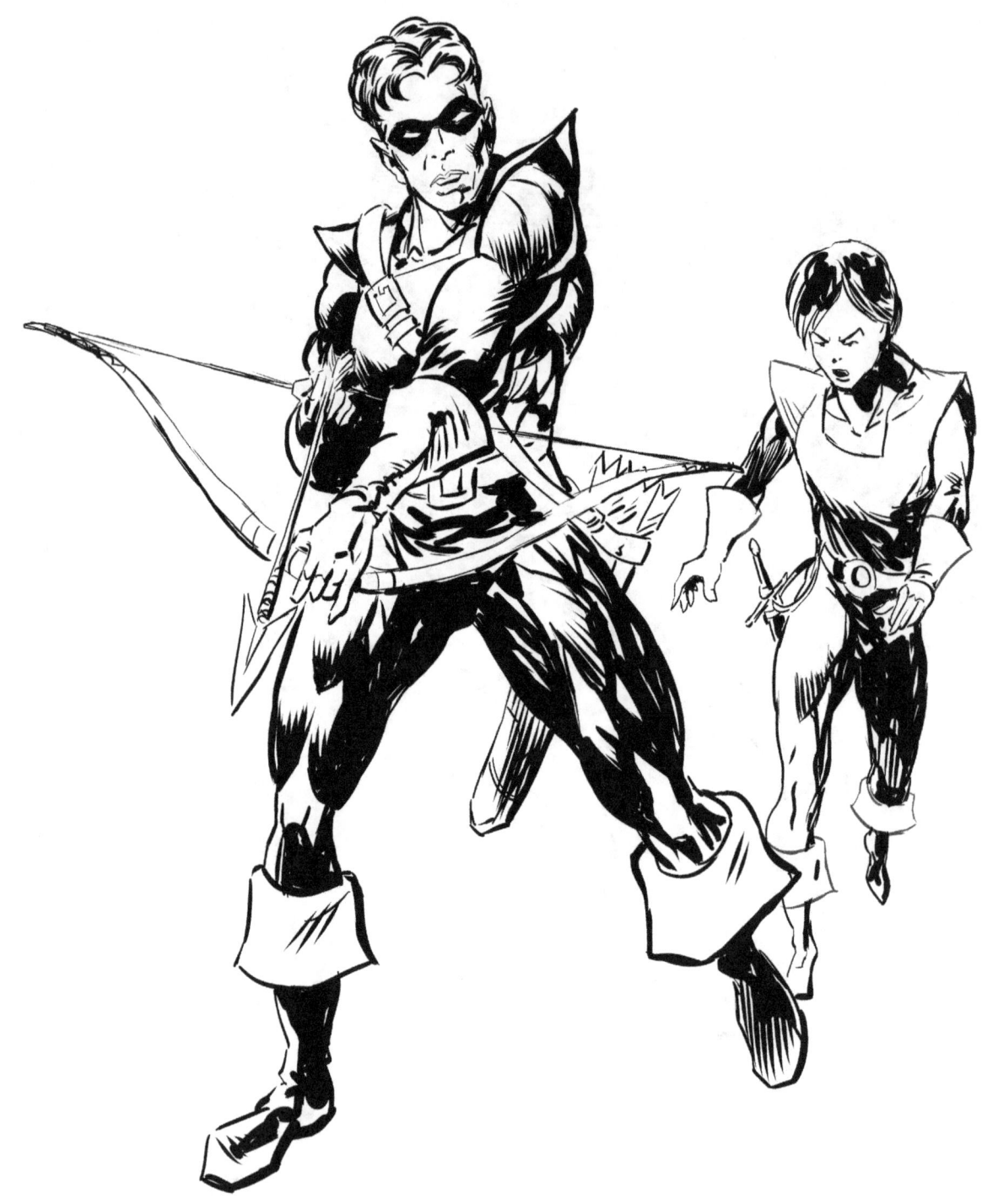

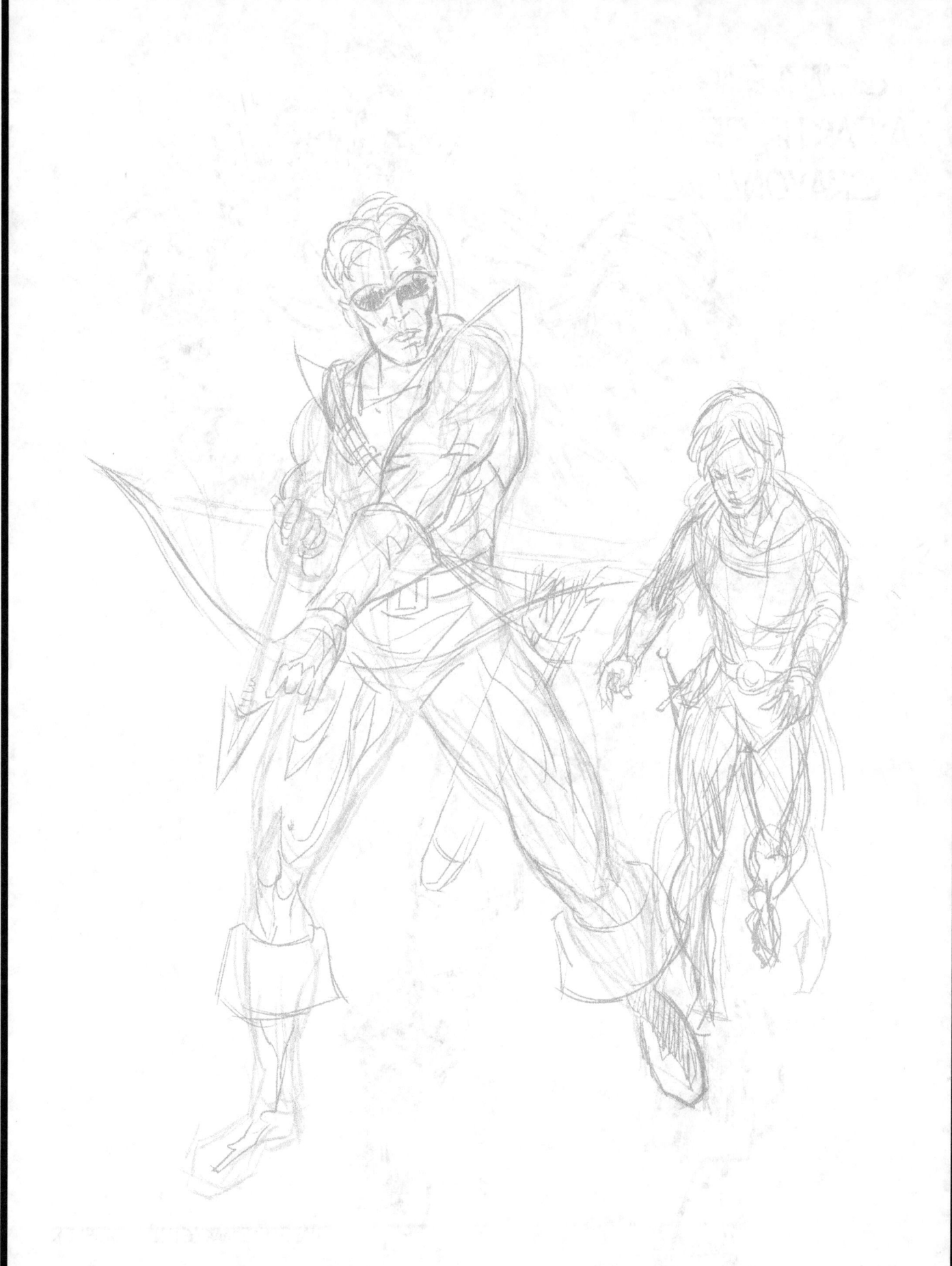

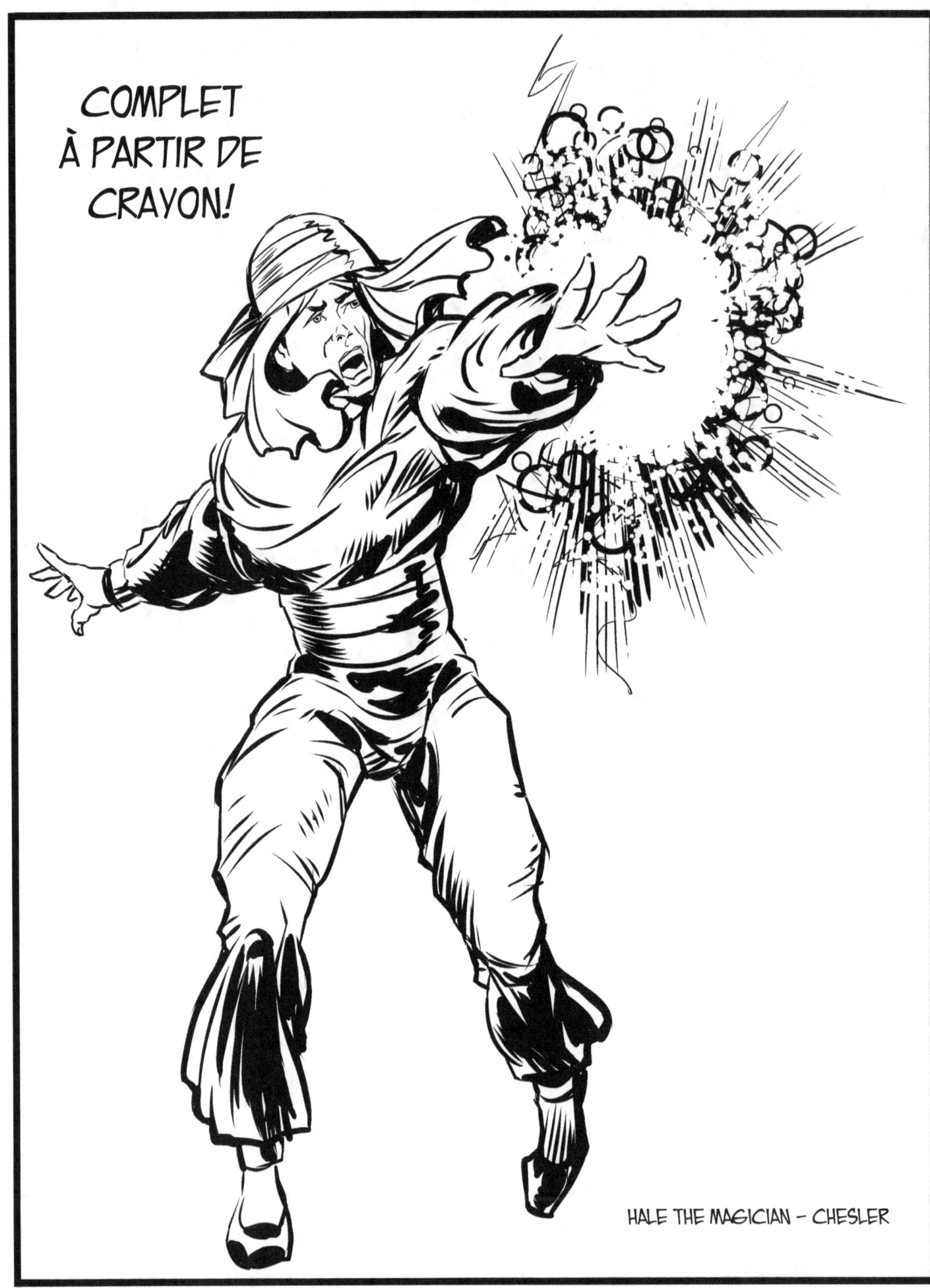

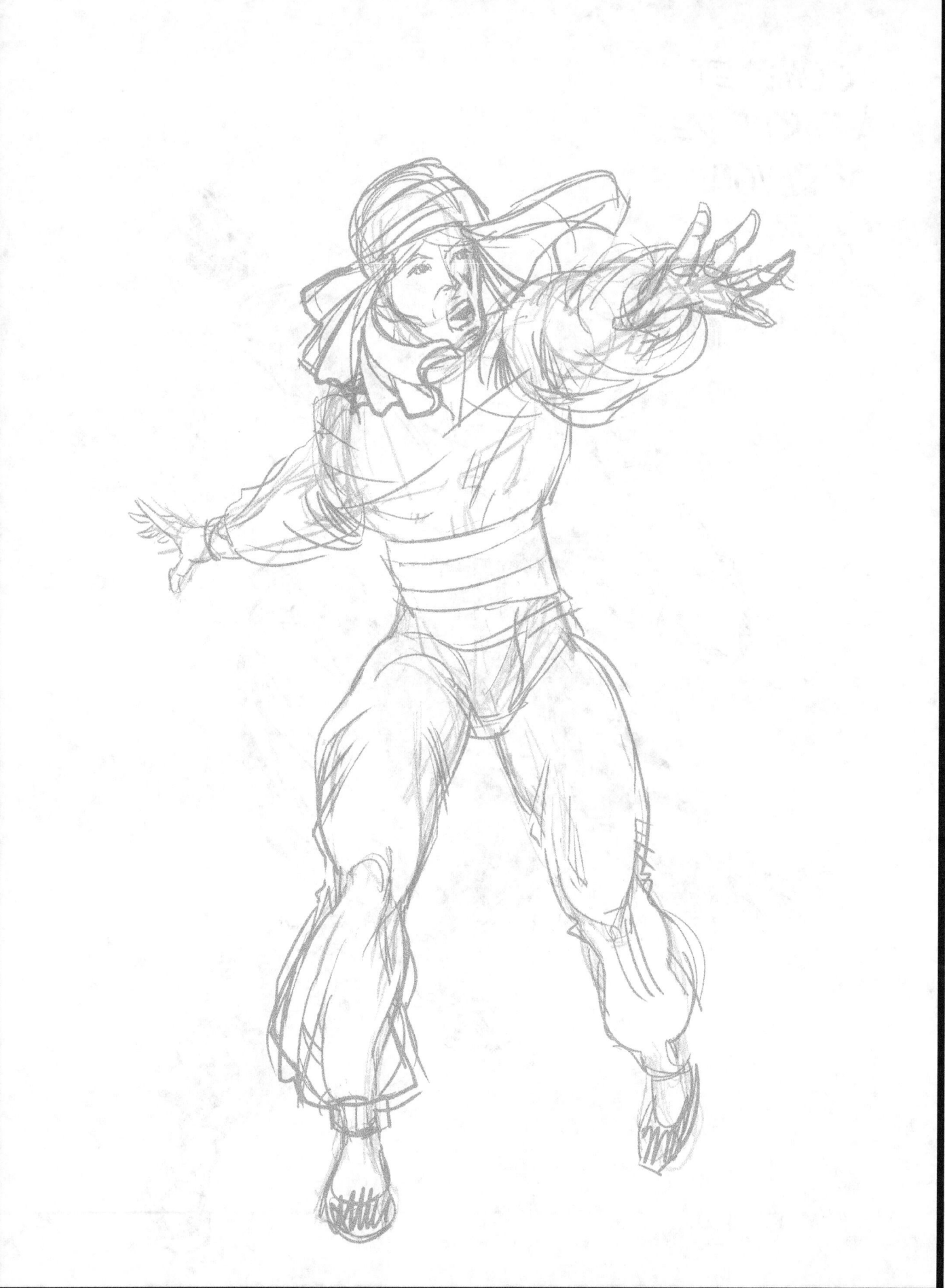

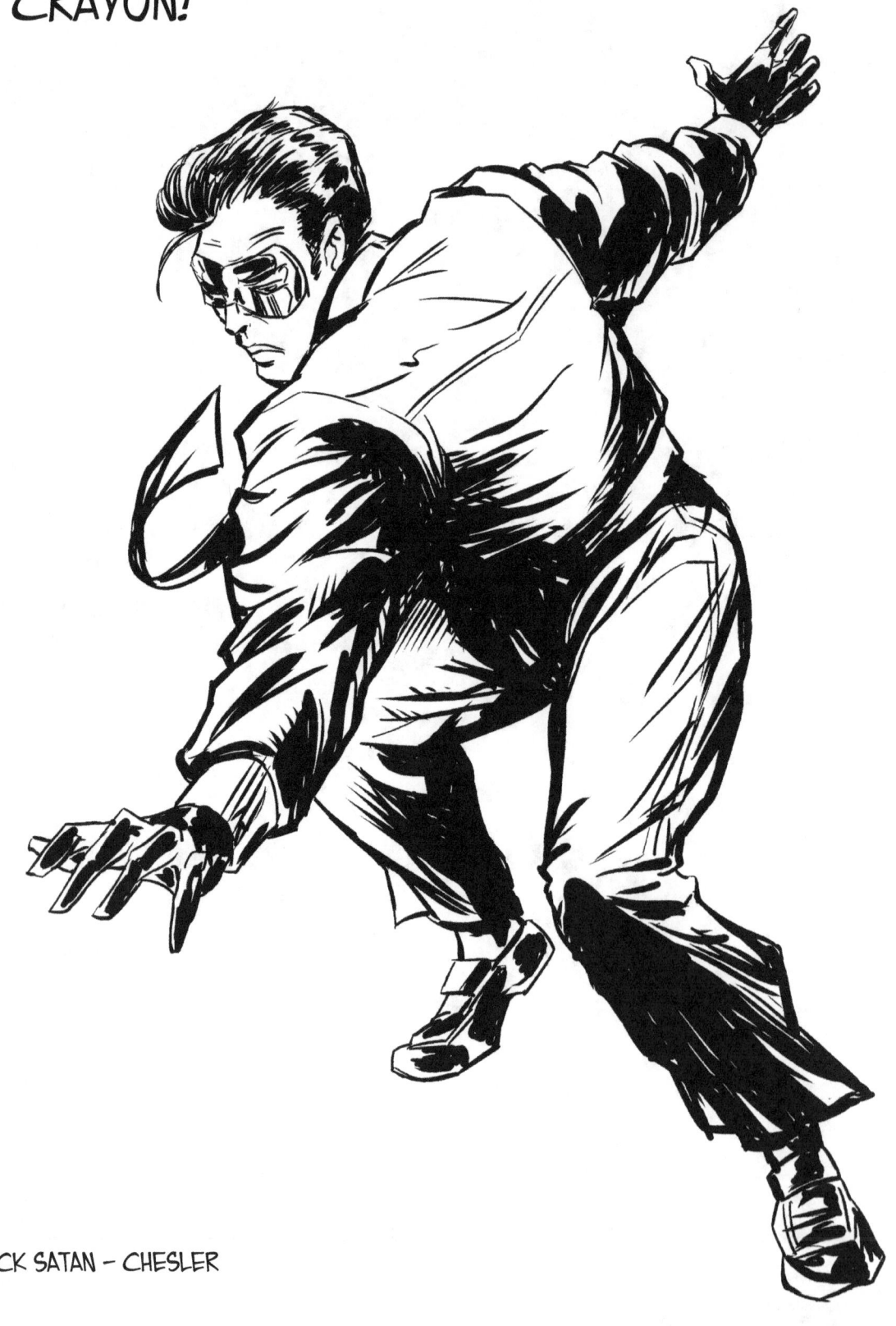

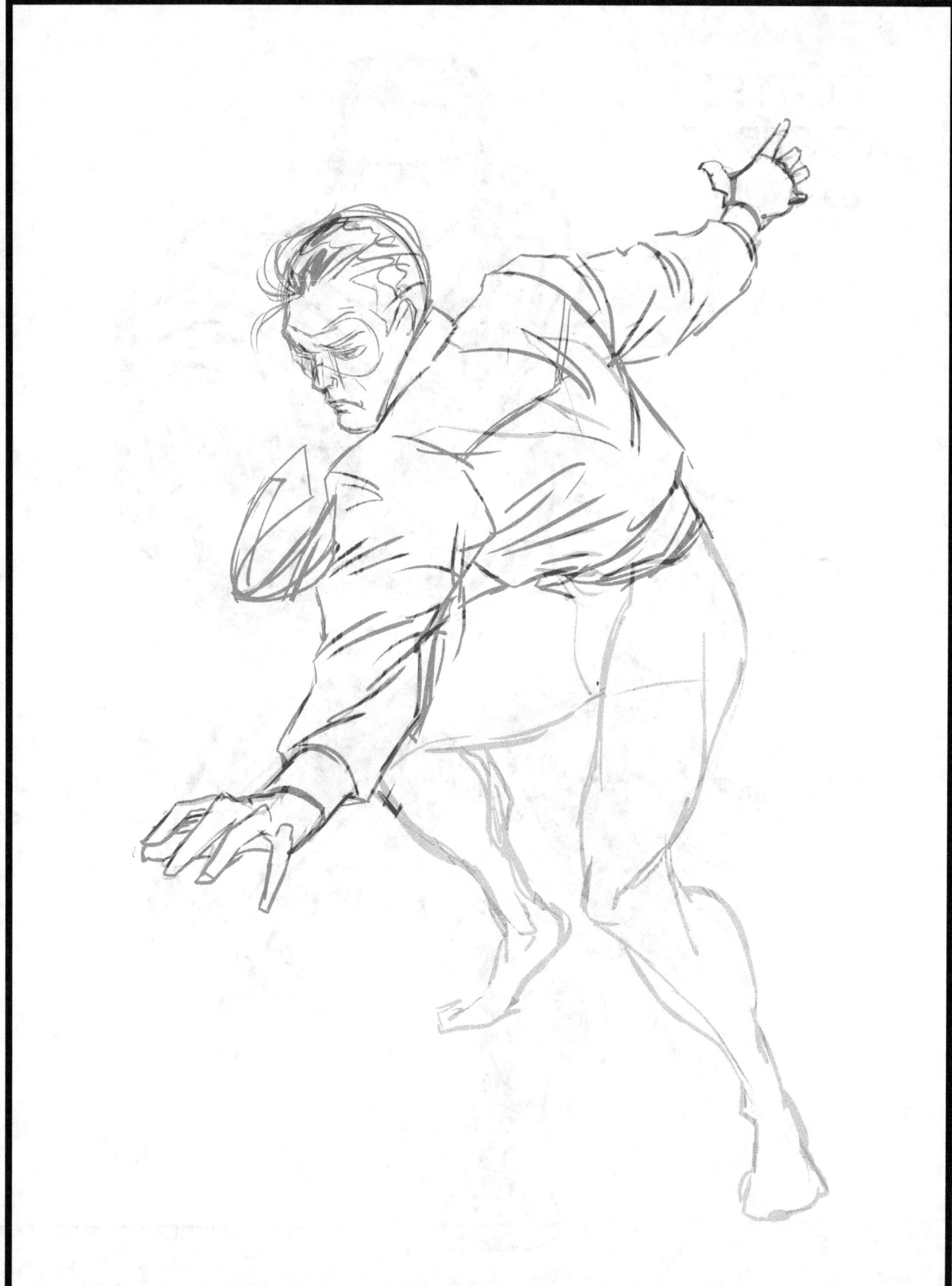

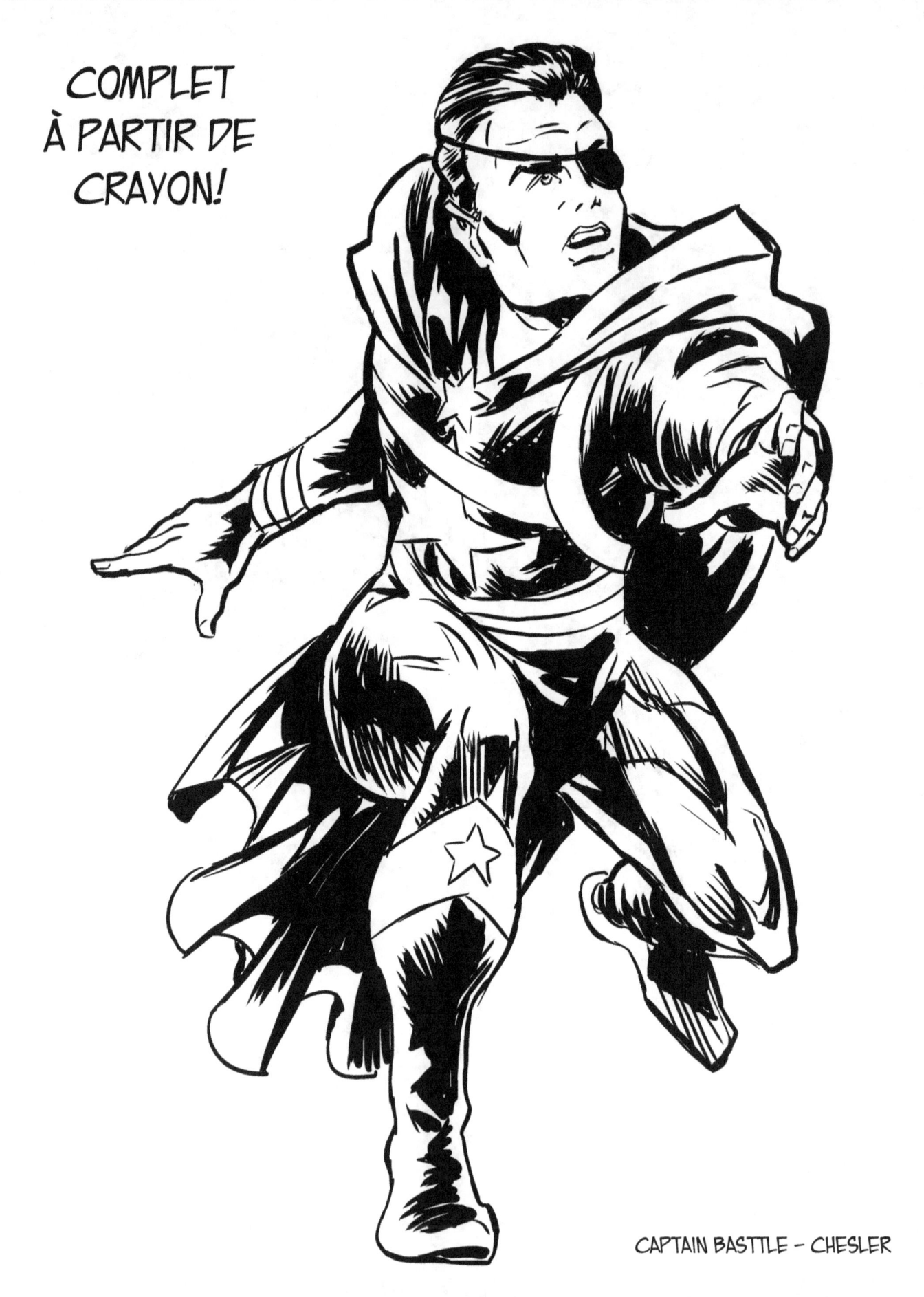

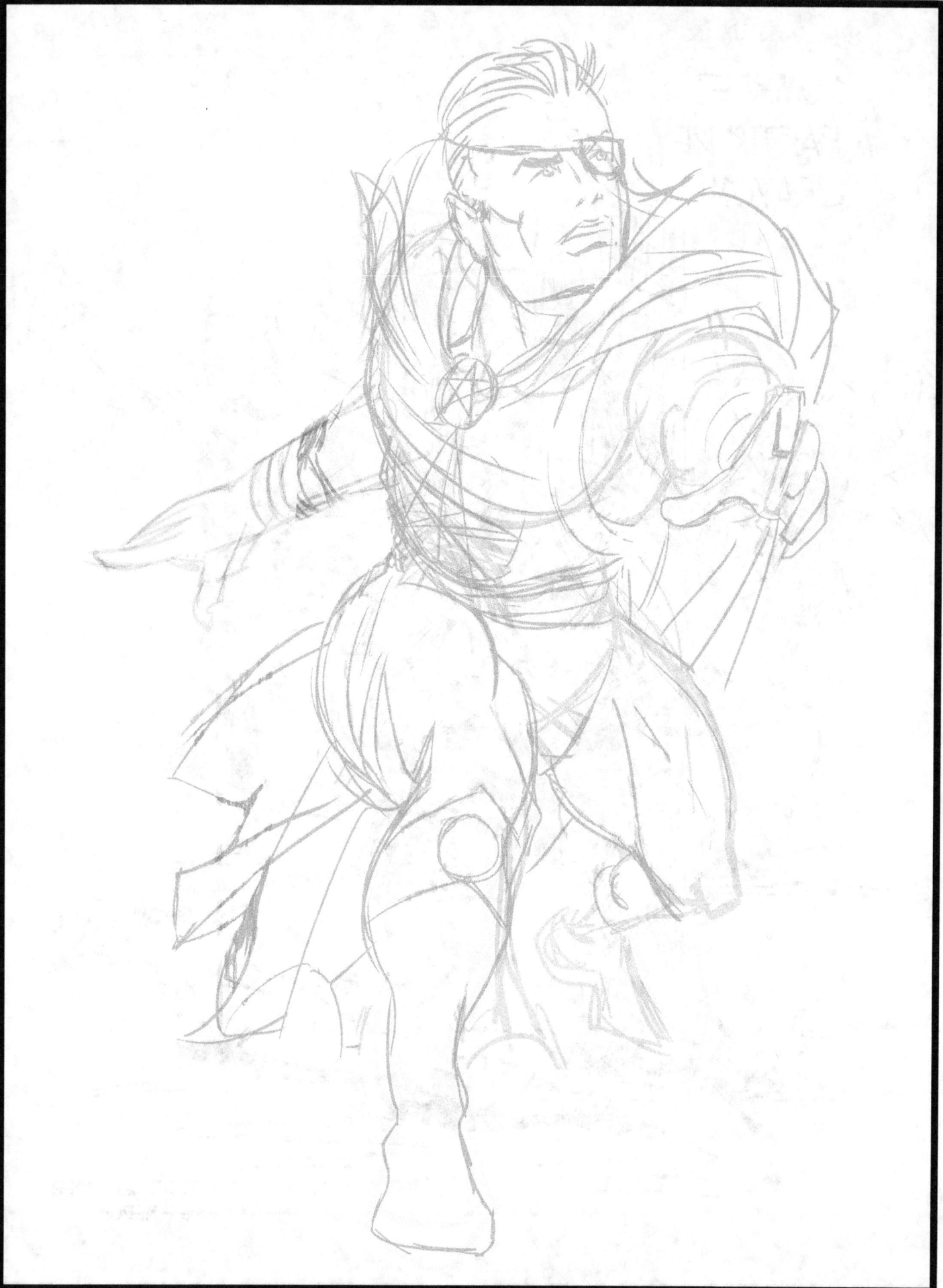

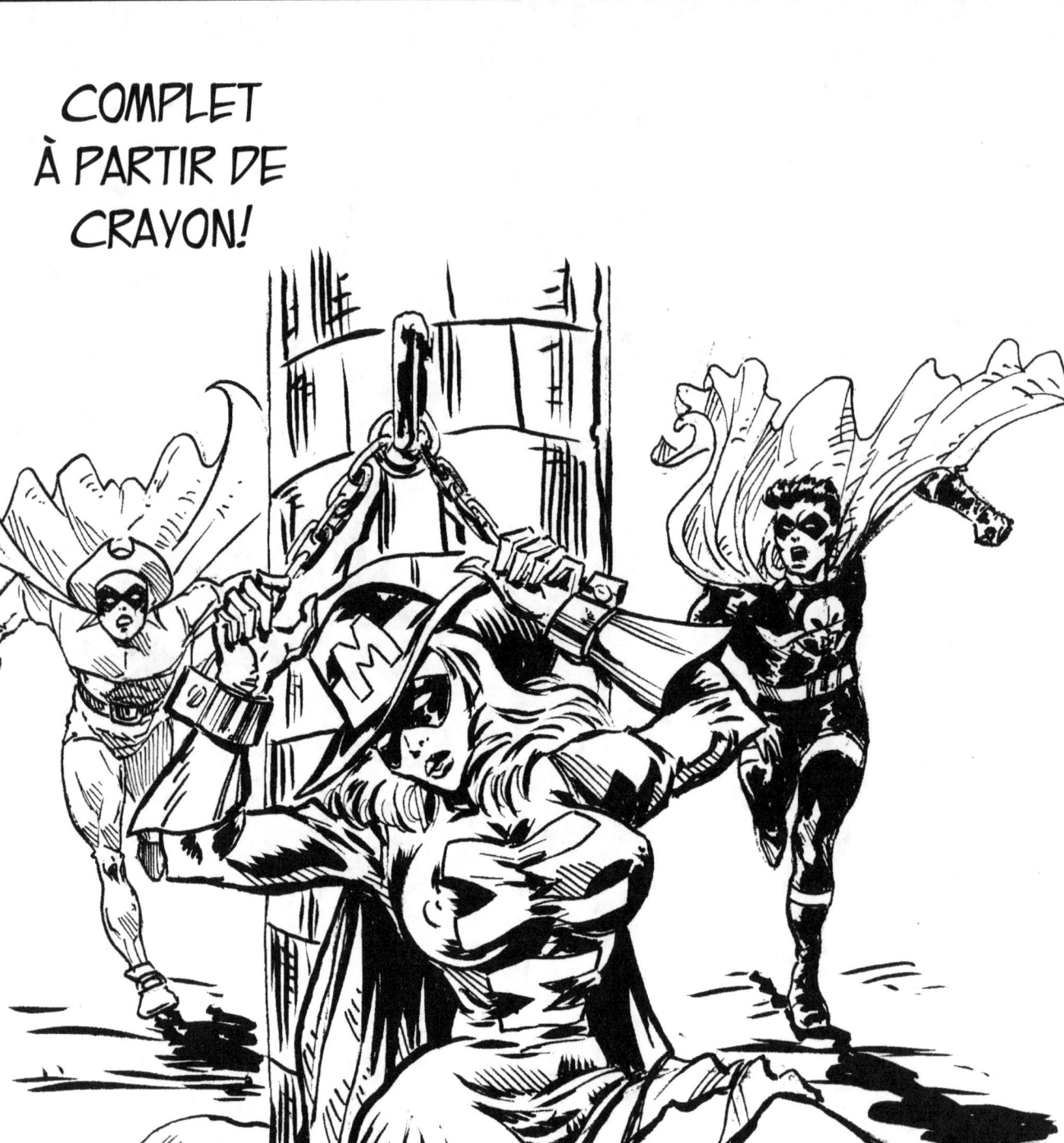

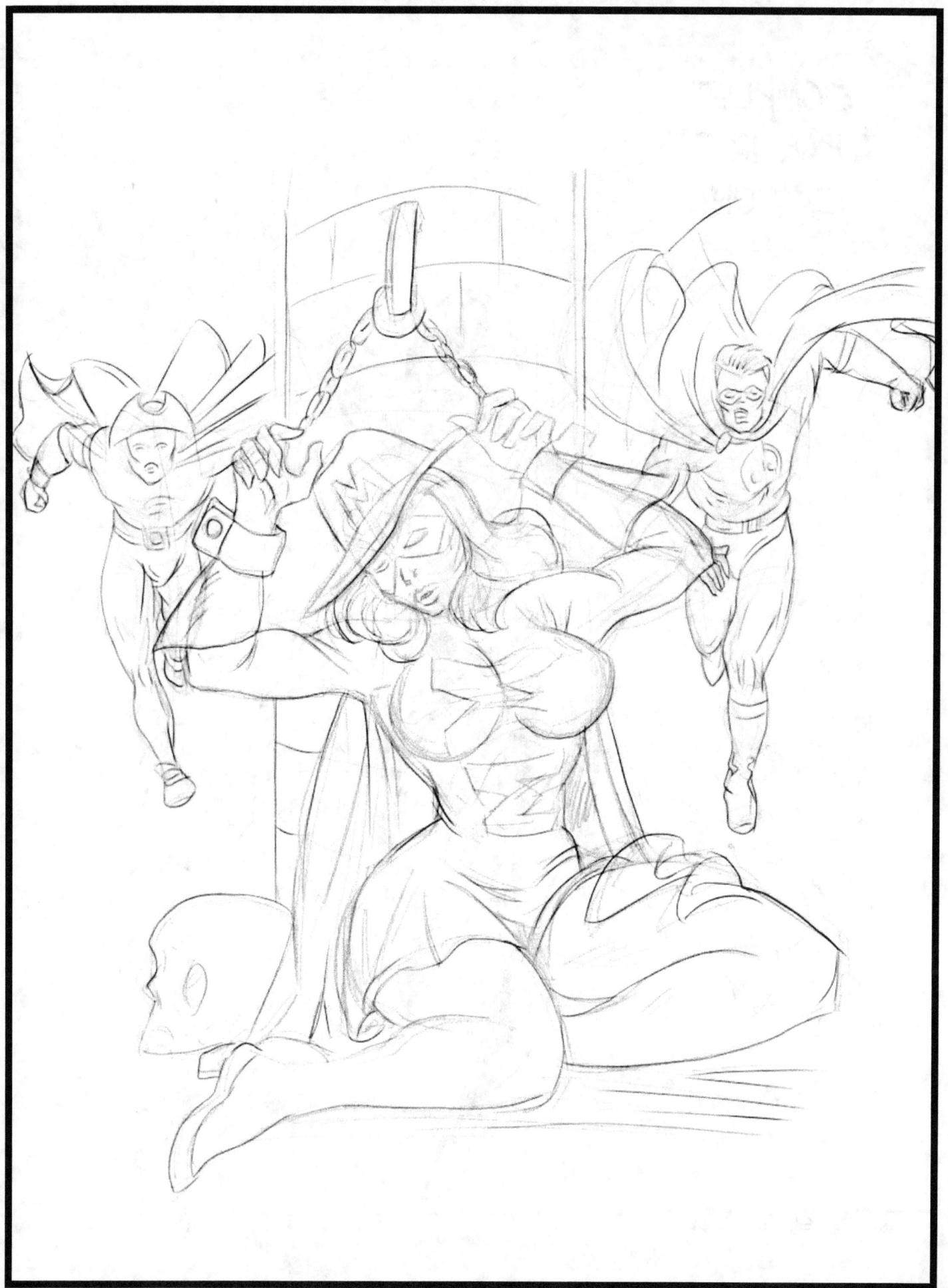

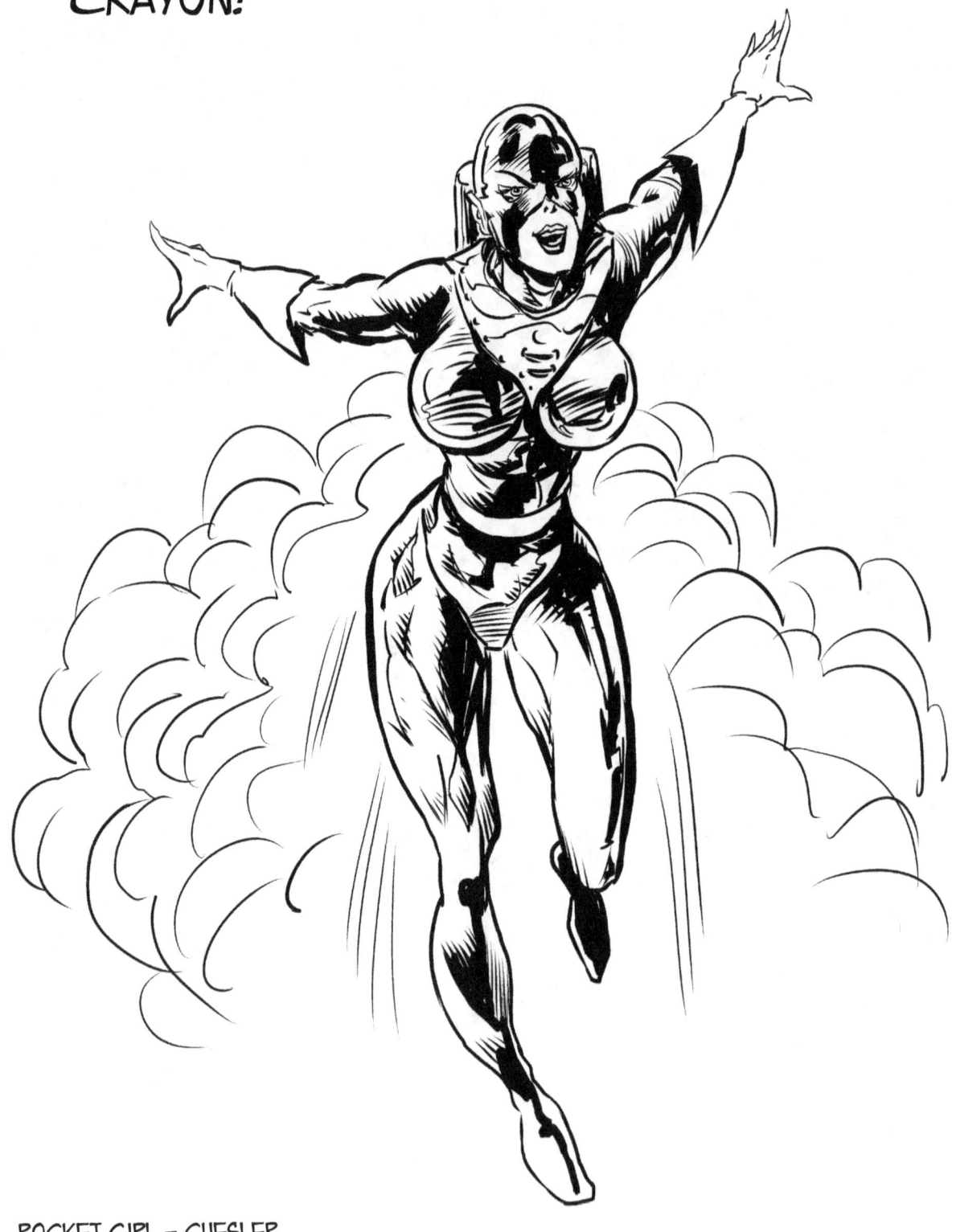

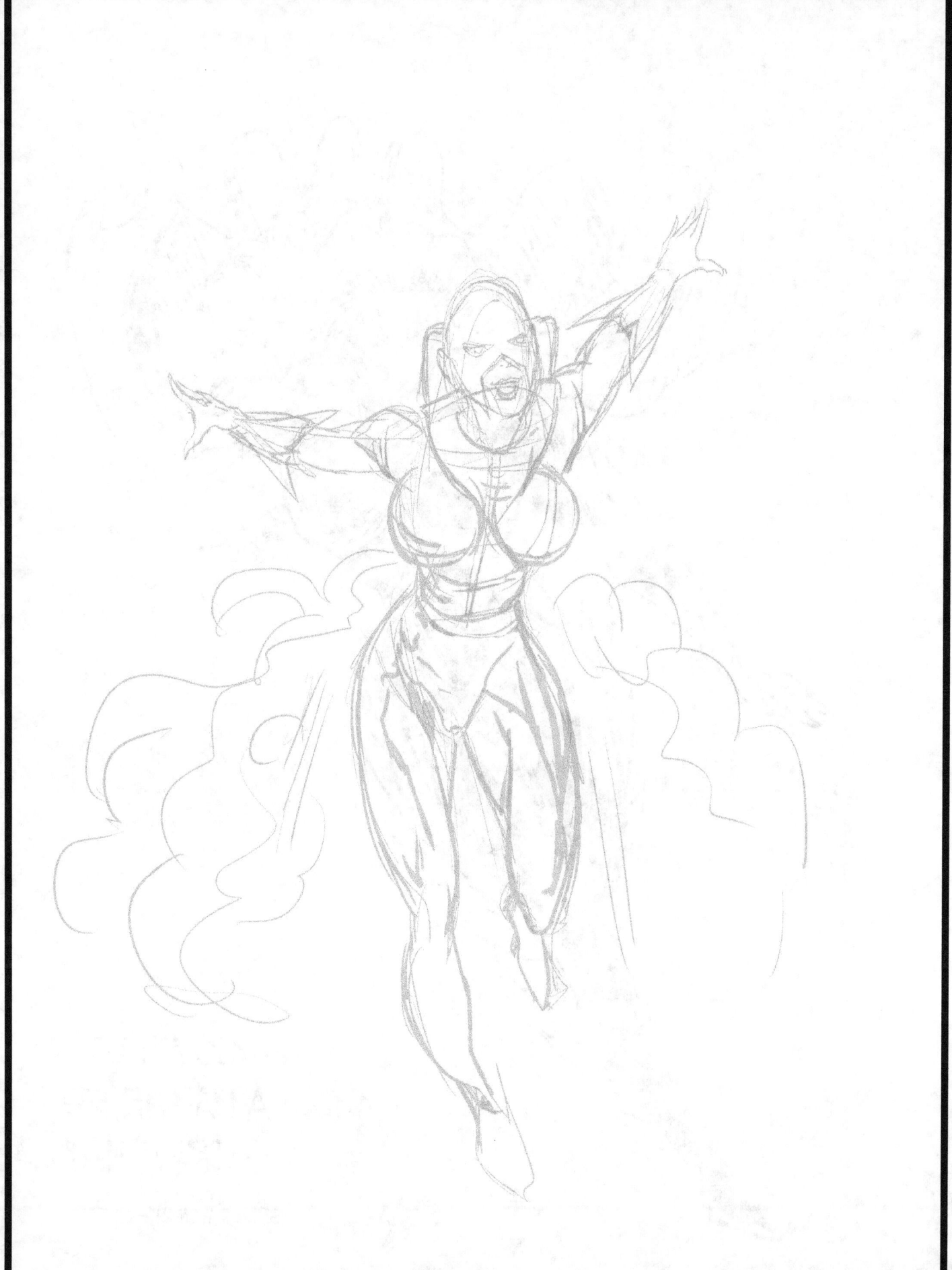

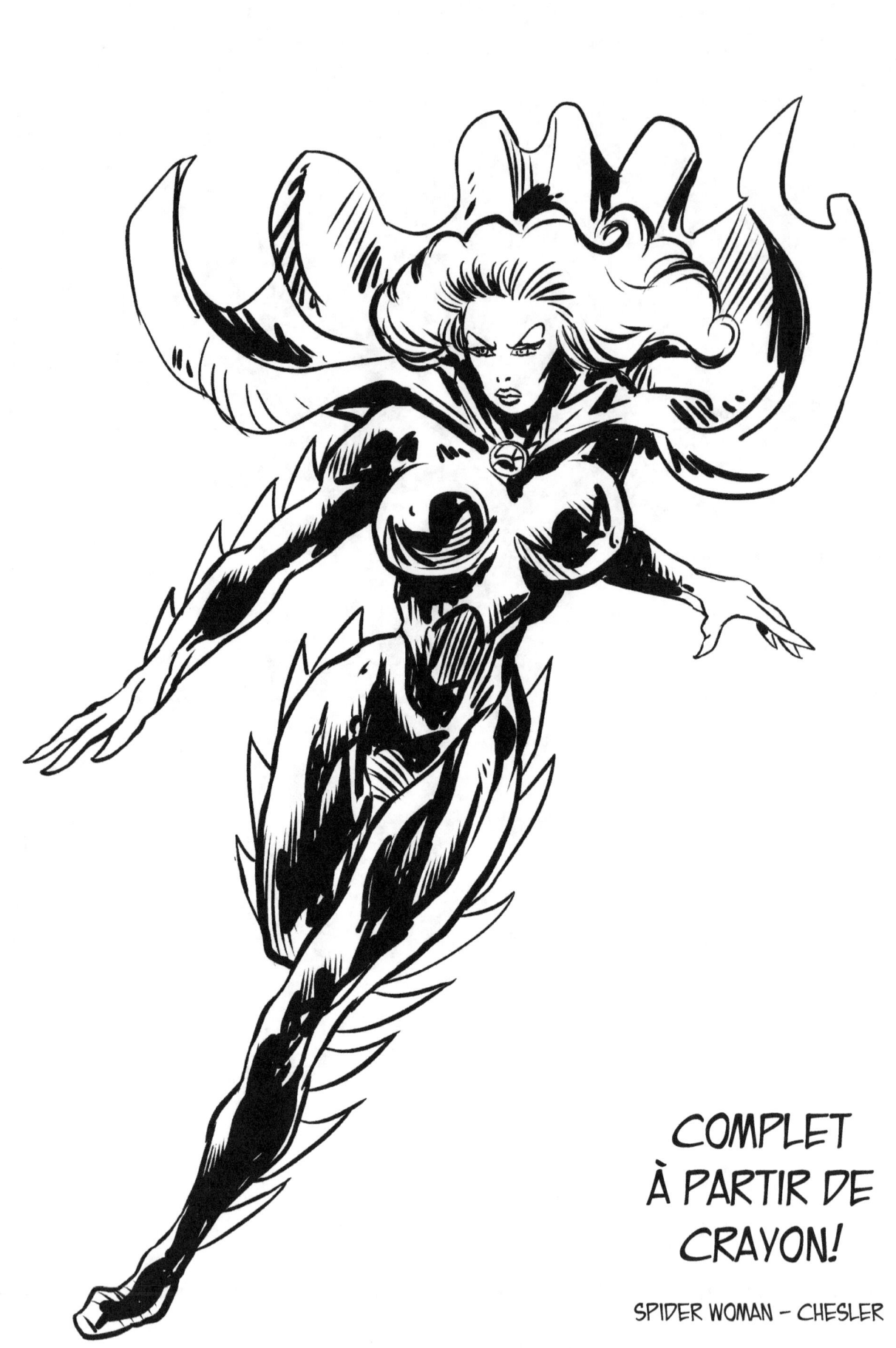

COMPLET À PARTIR DE CRAYON!

SPIDER WOMAN – CHESLER

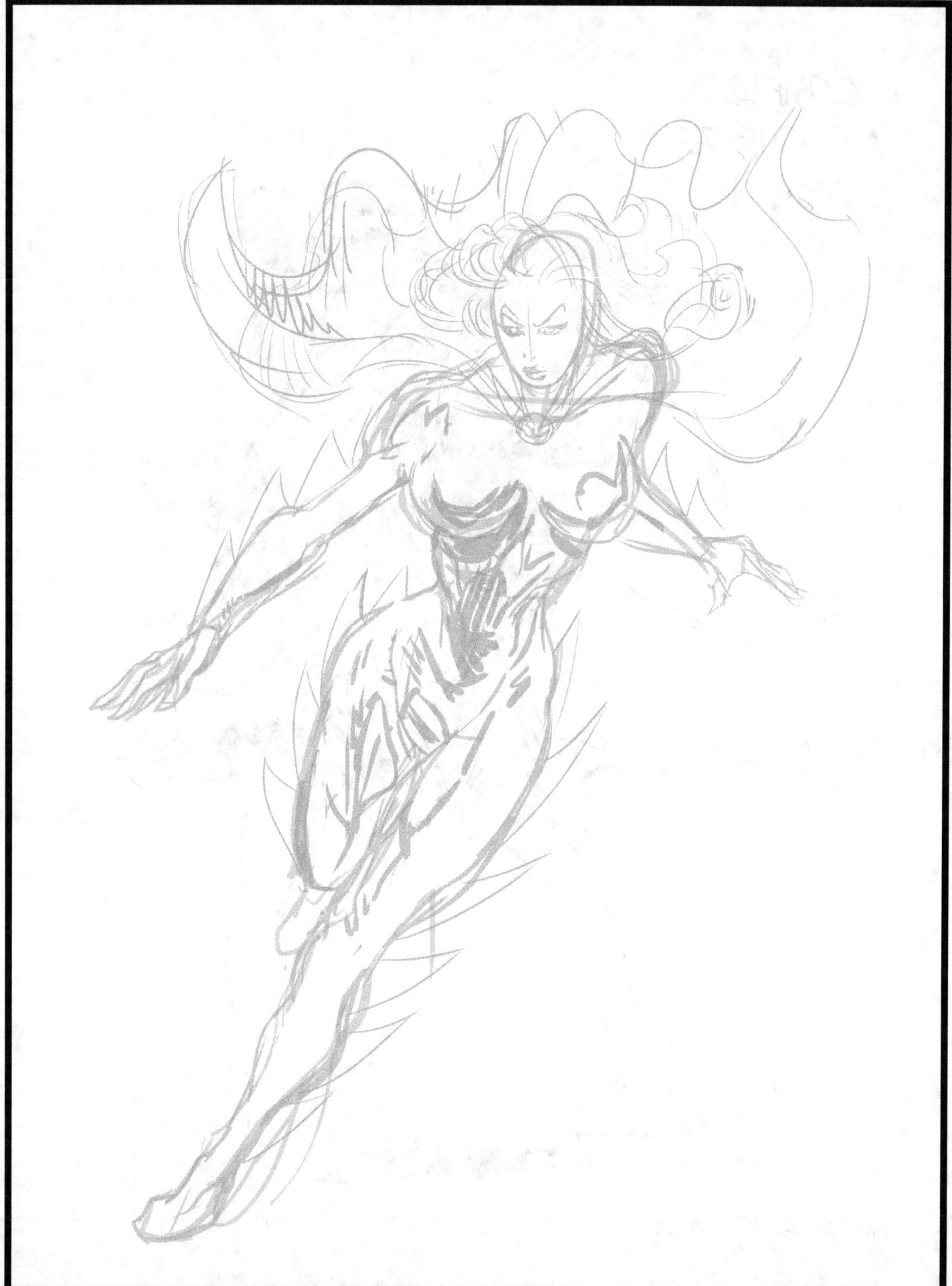

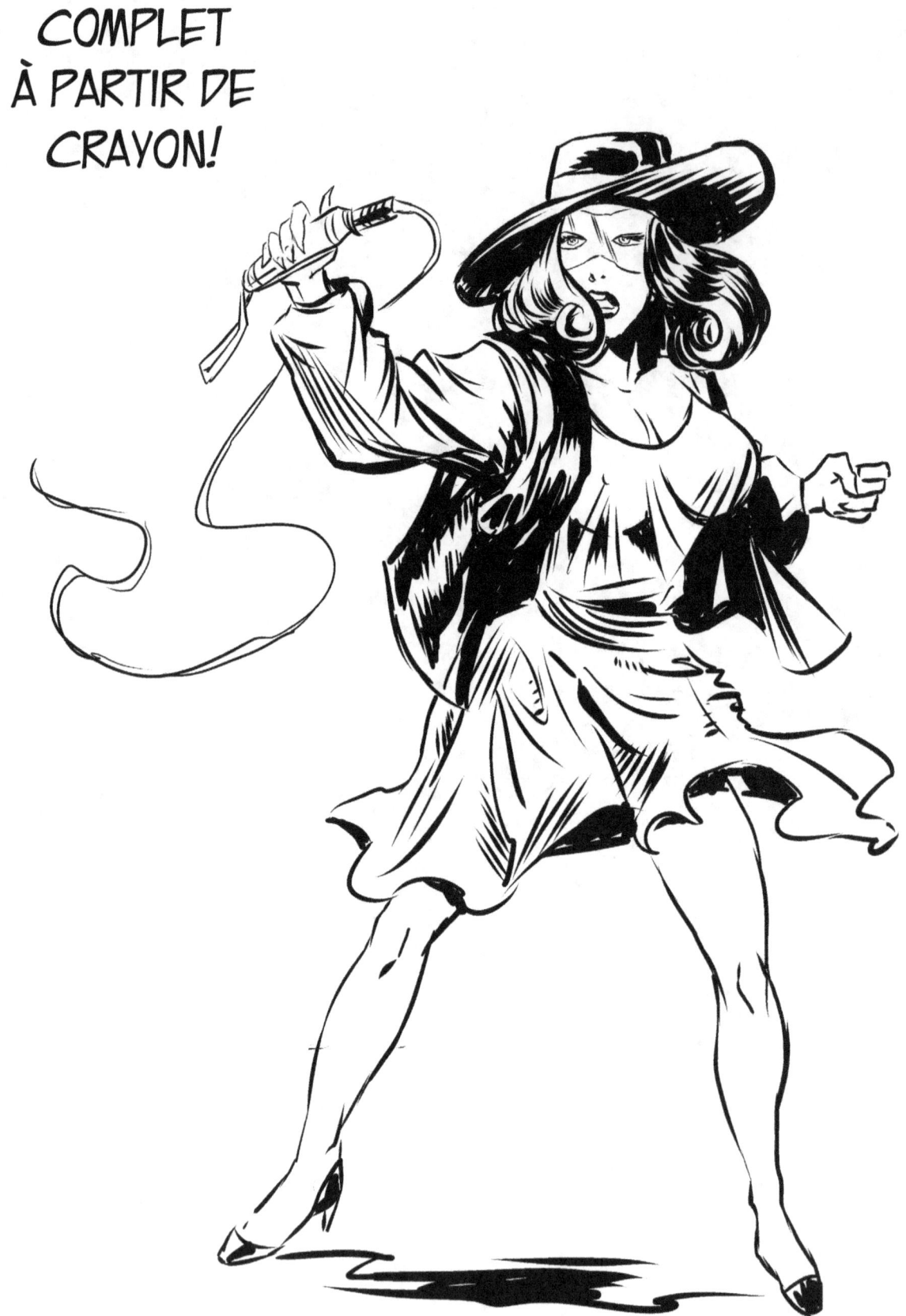

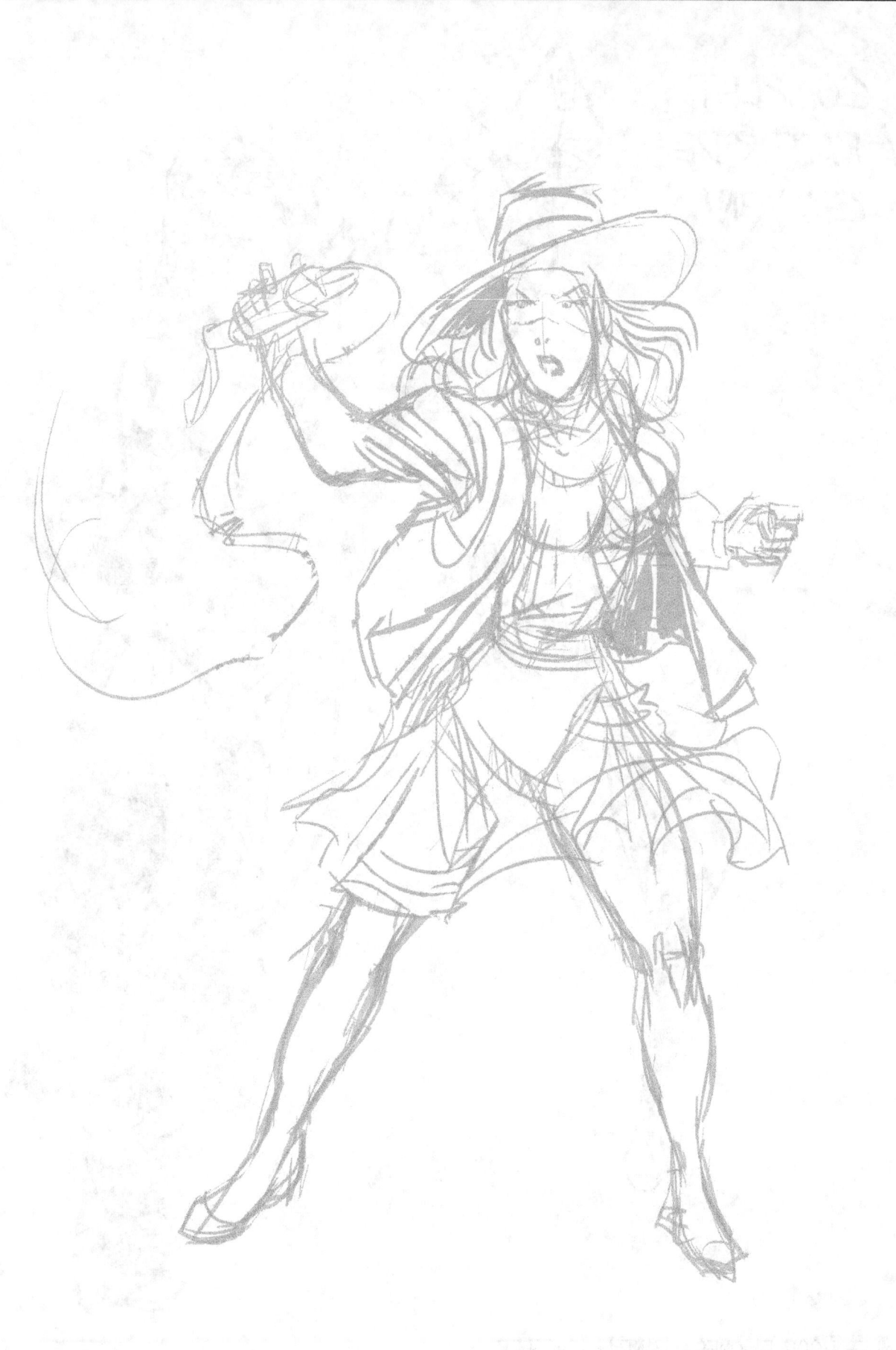

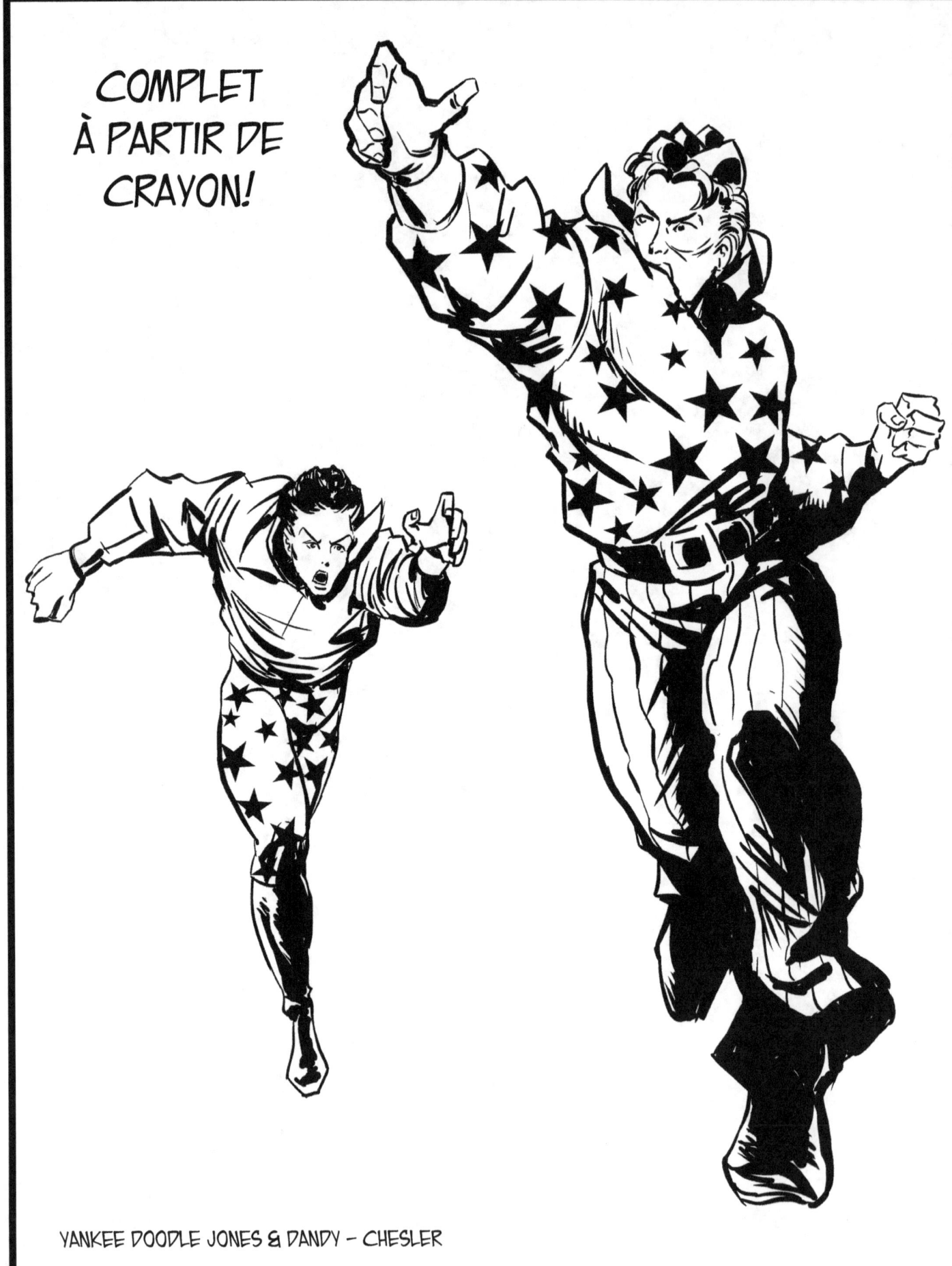

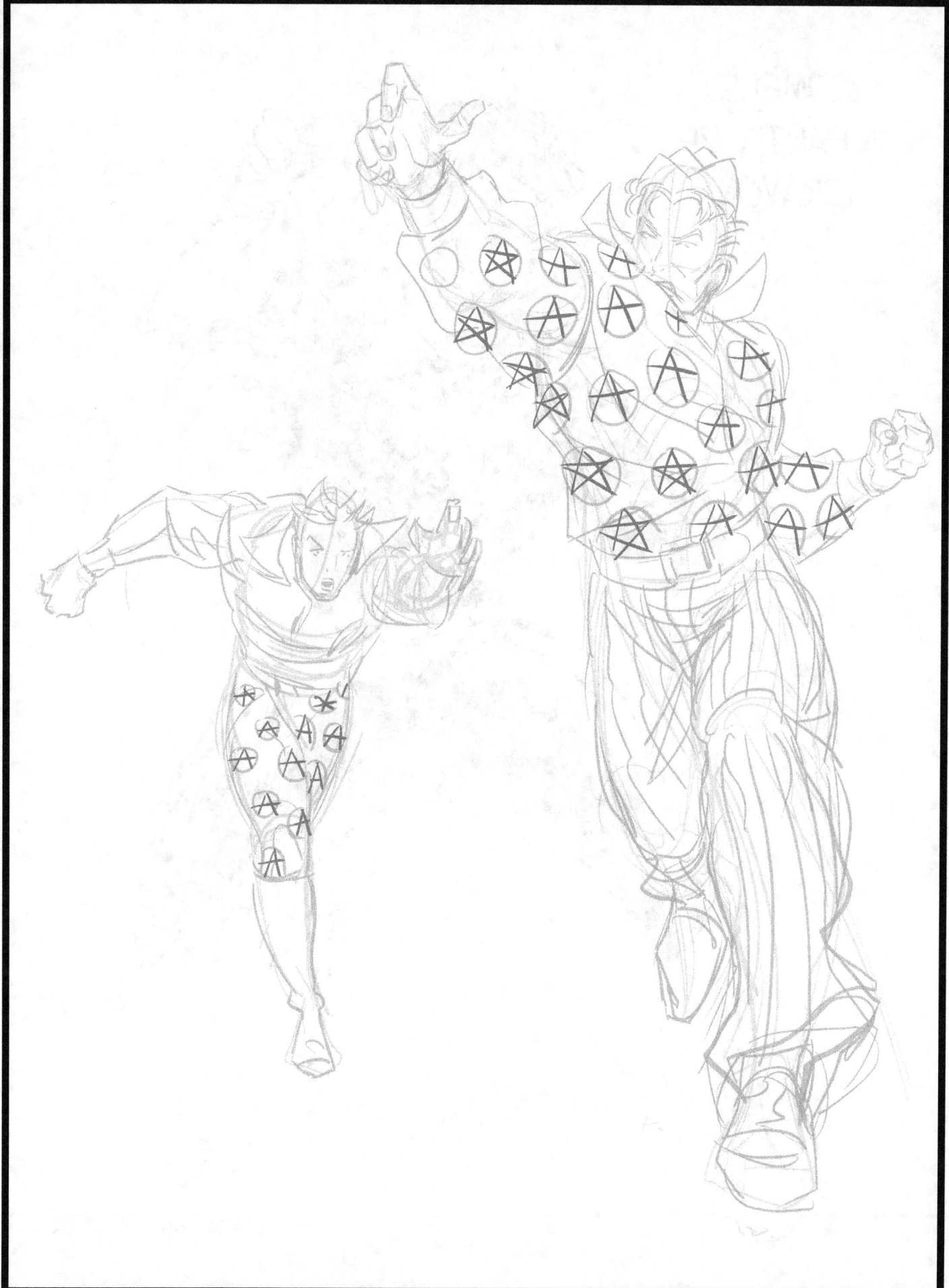

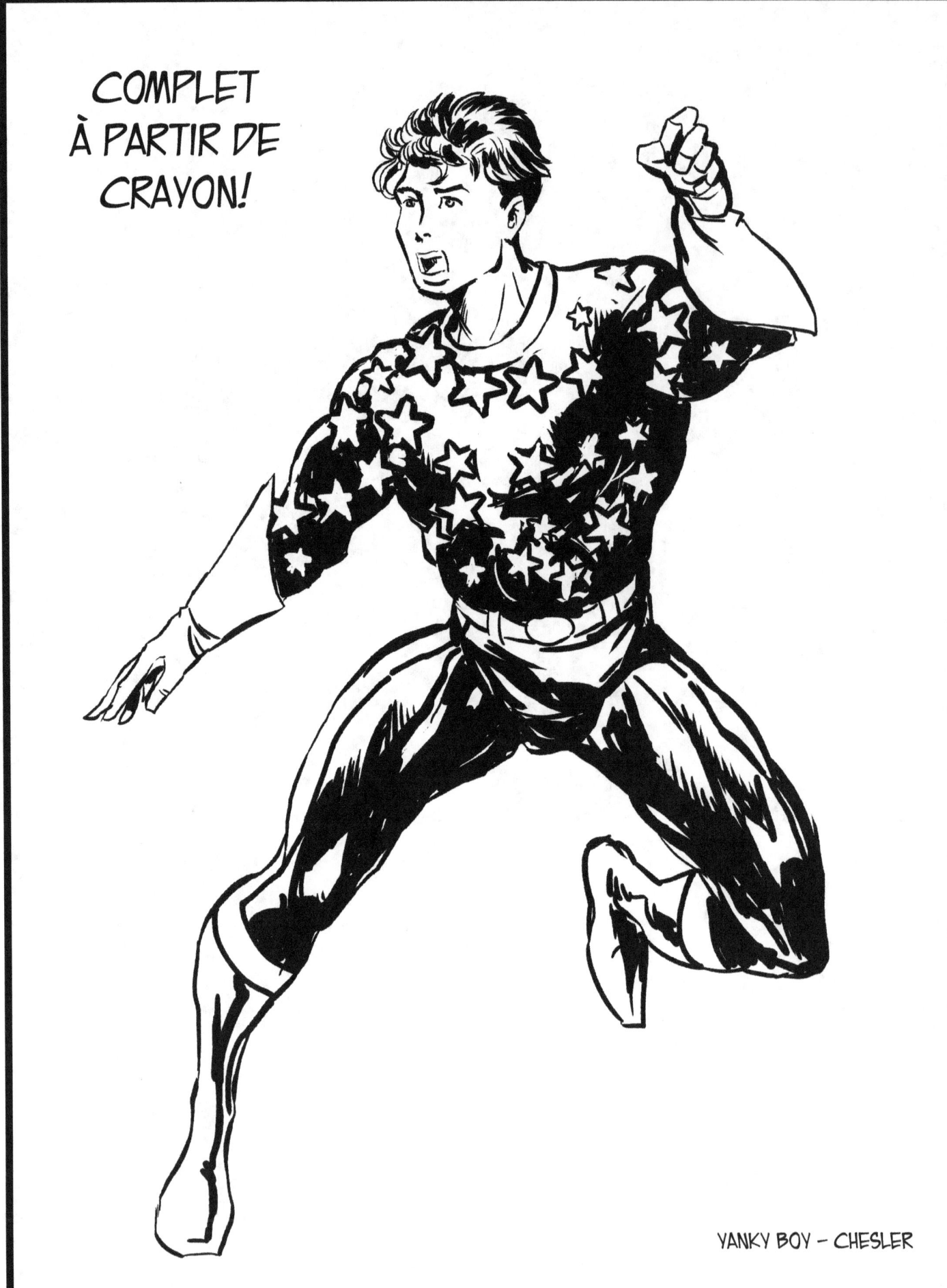

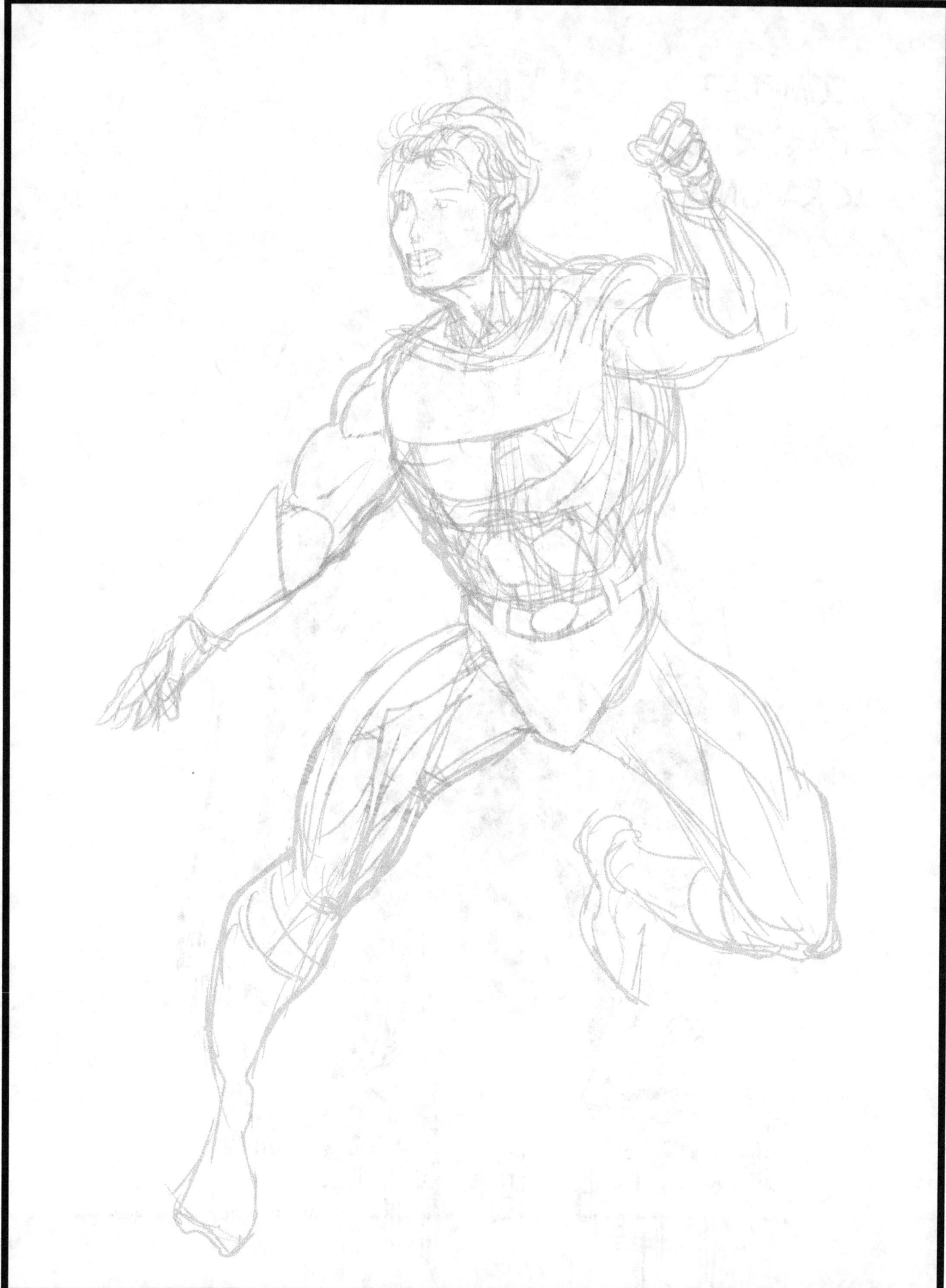

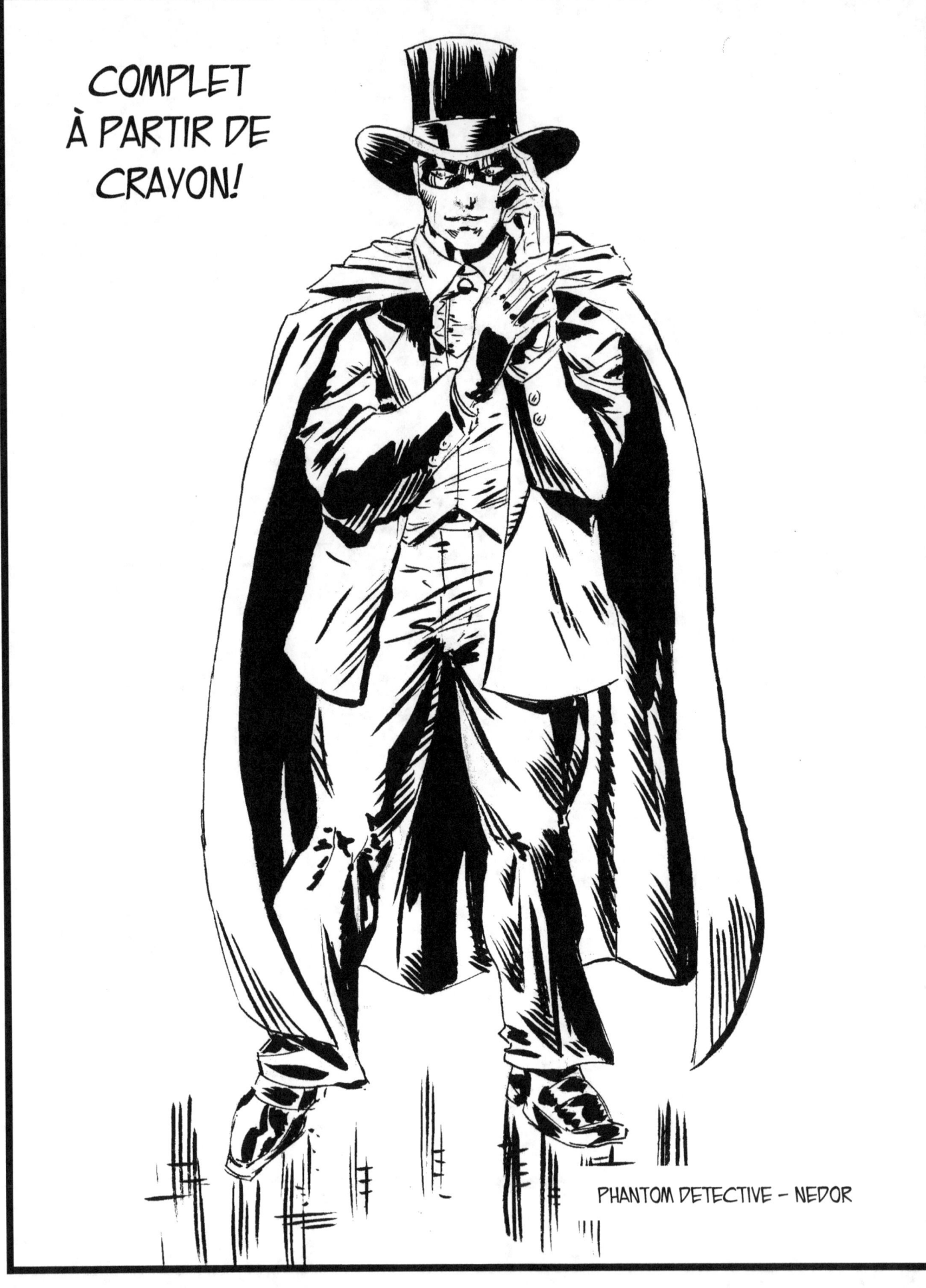

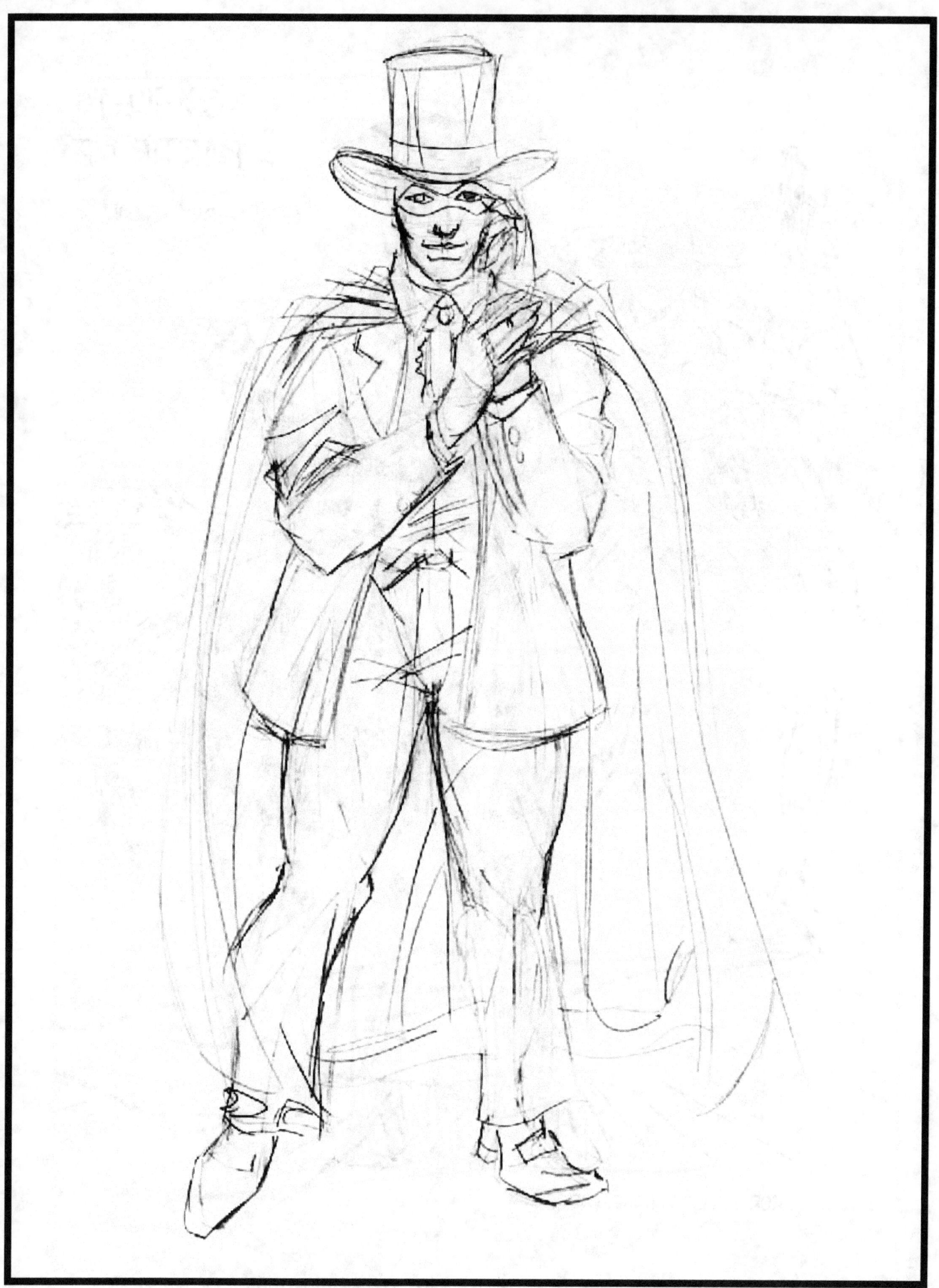

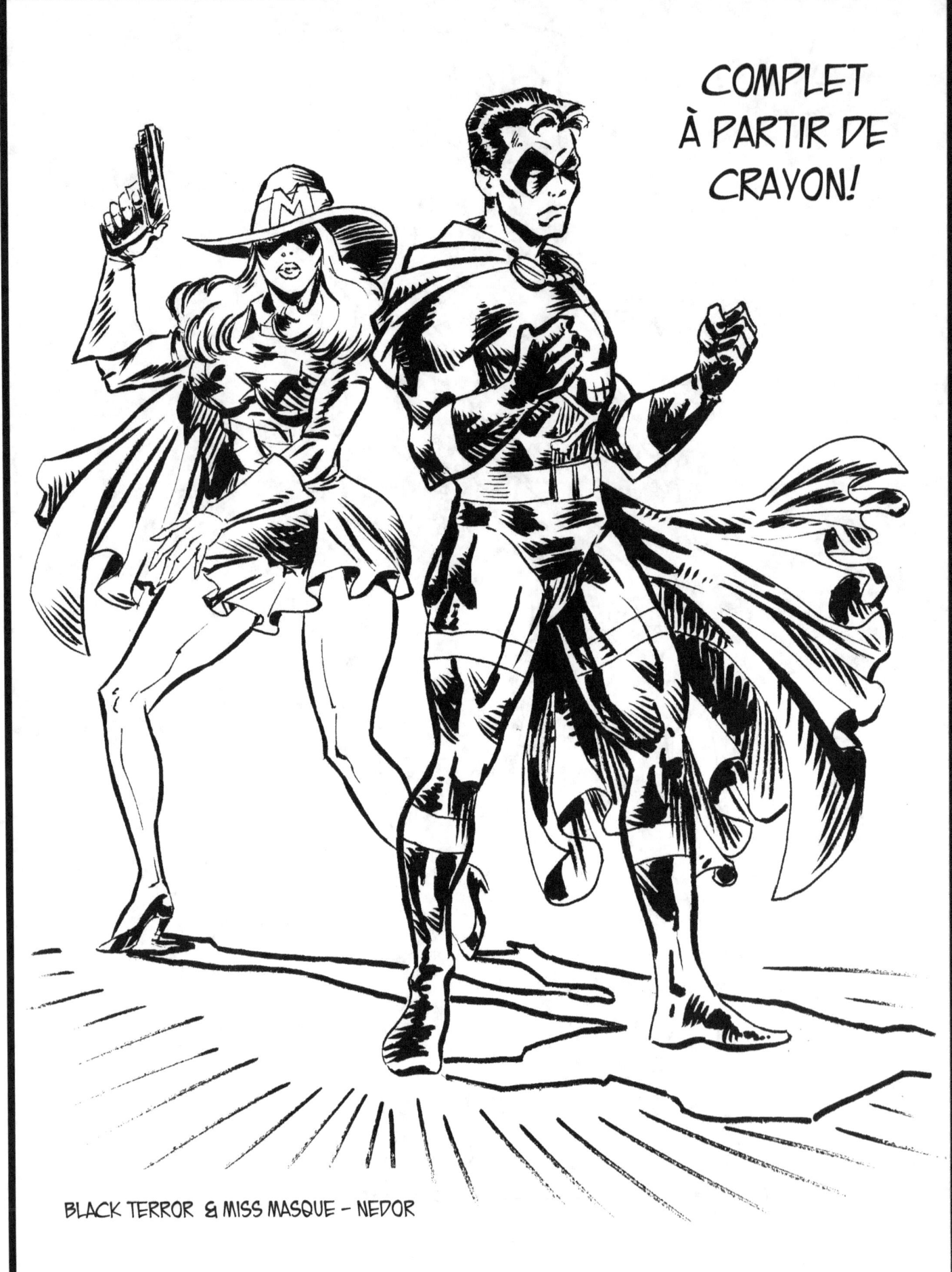

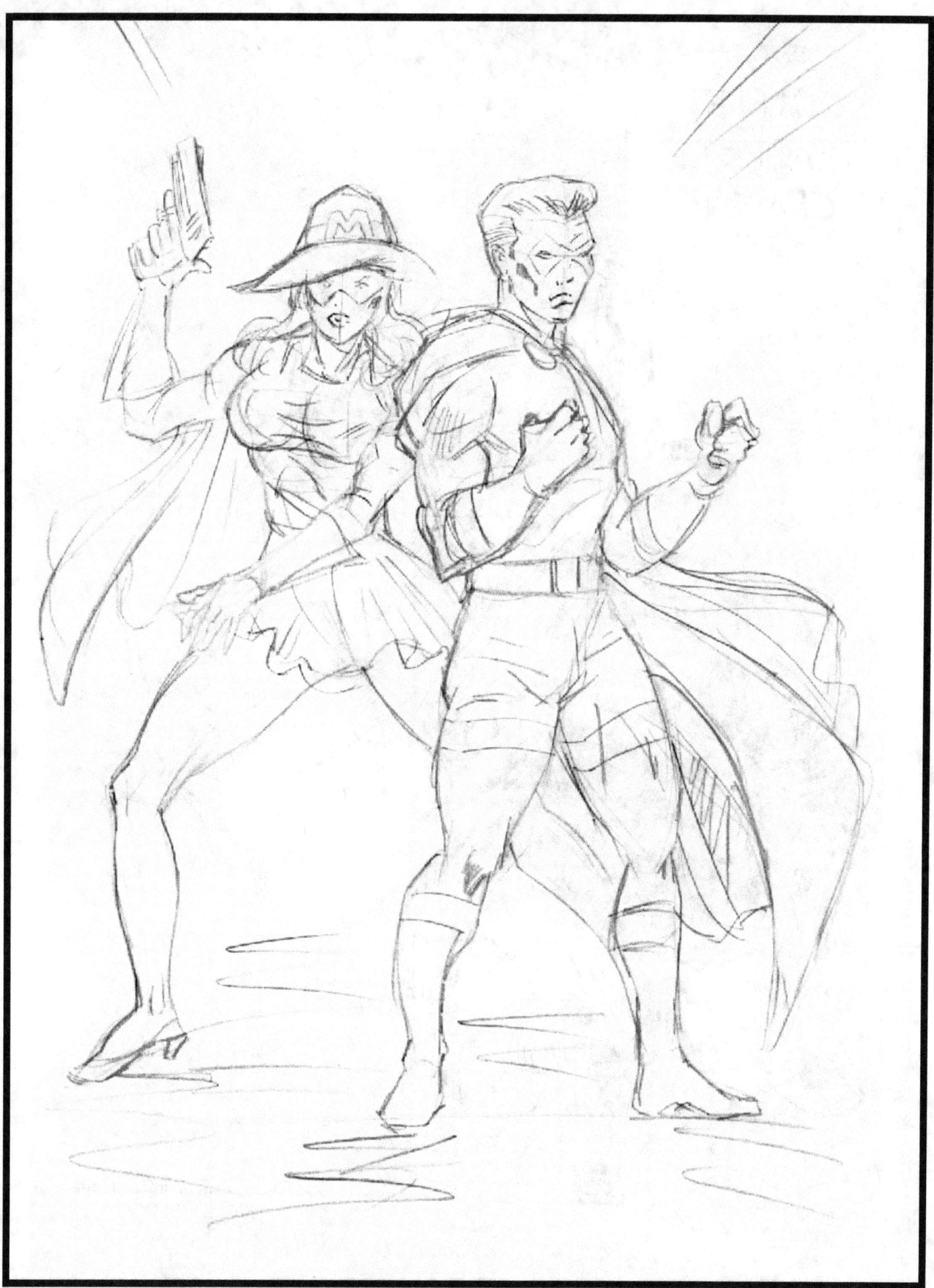

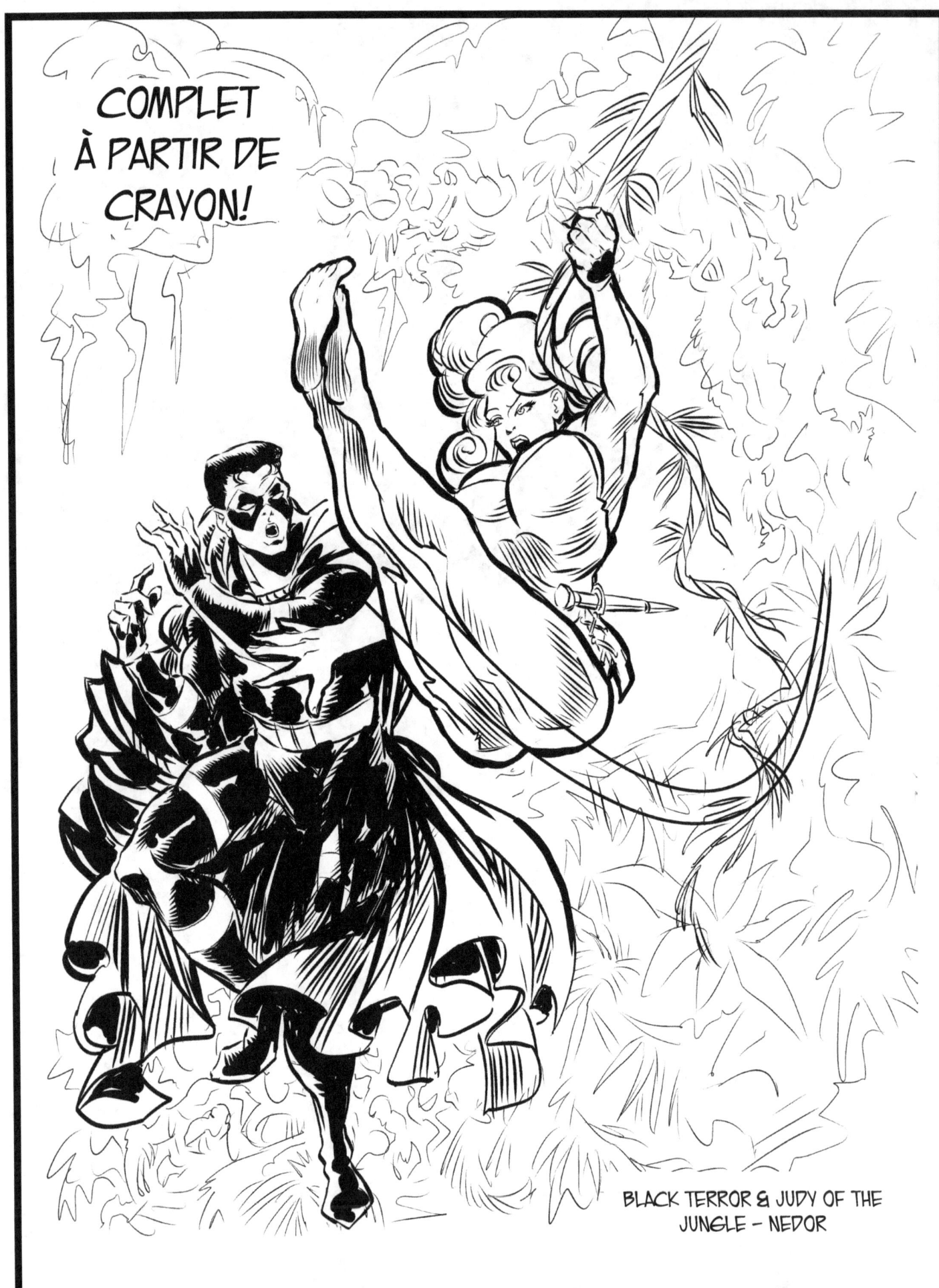

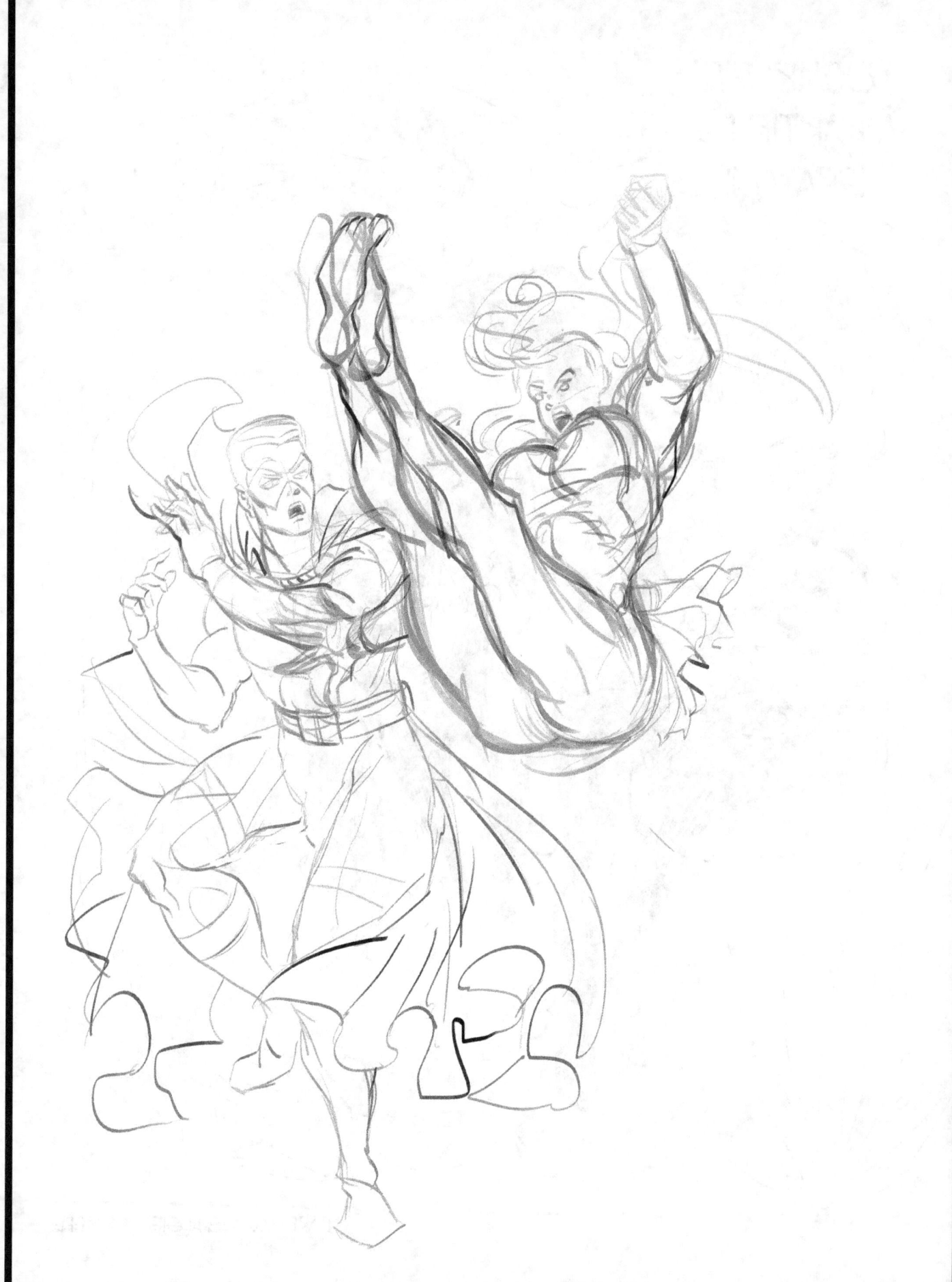

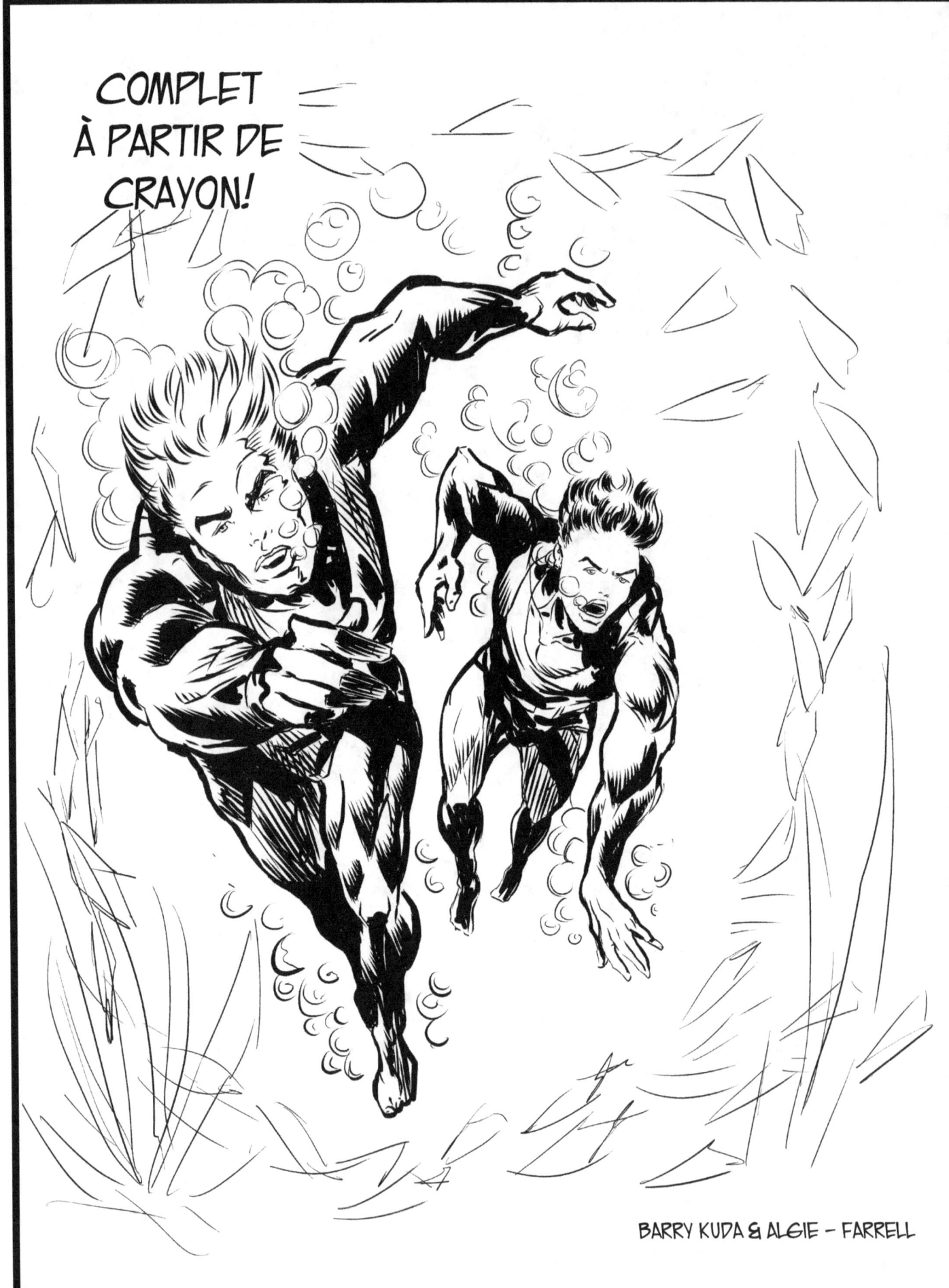

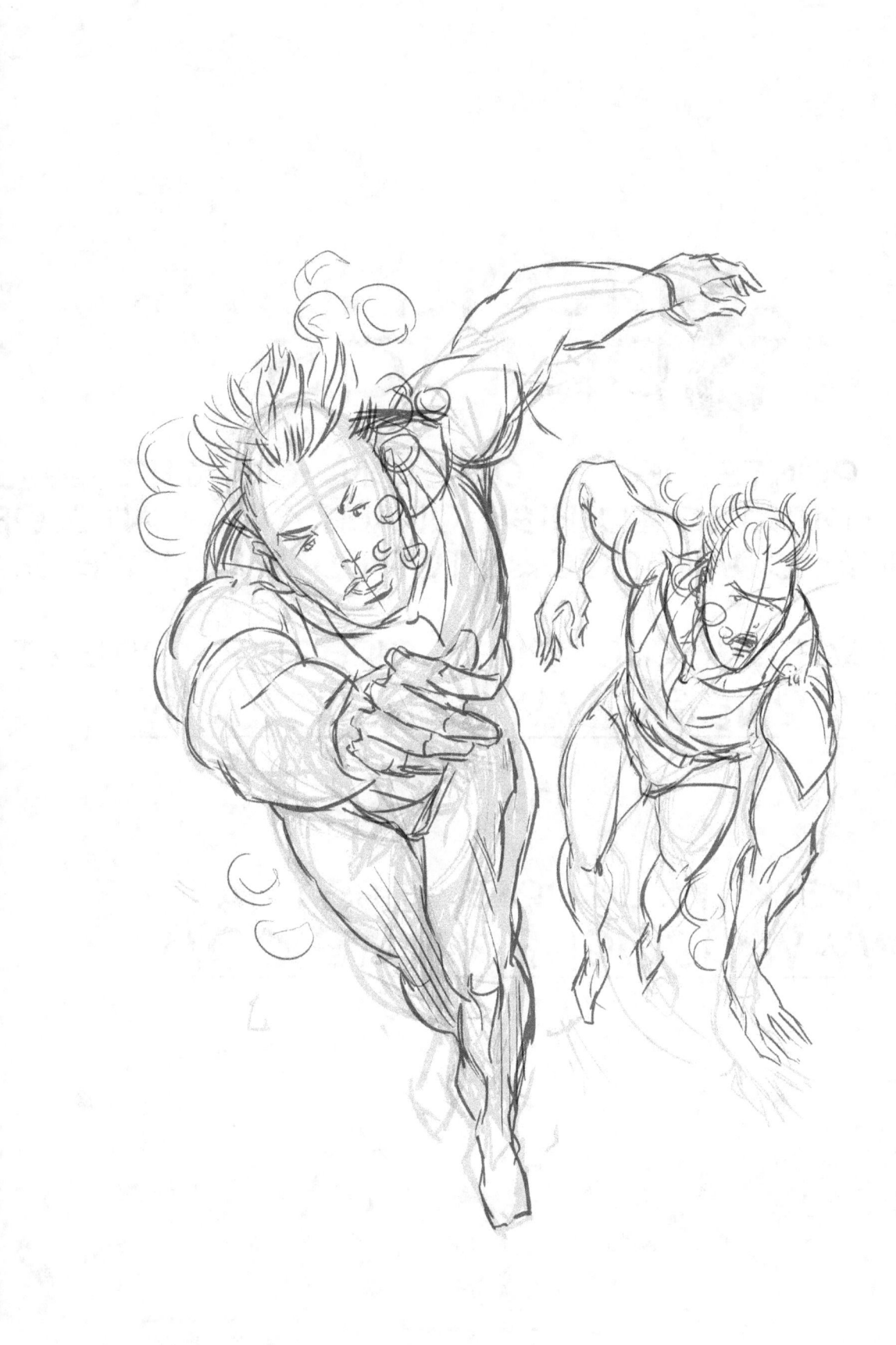

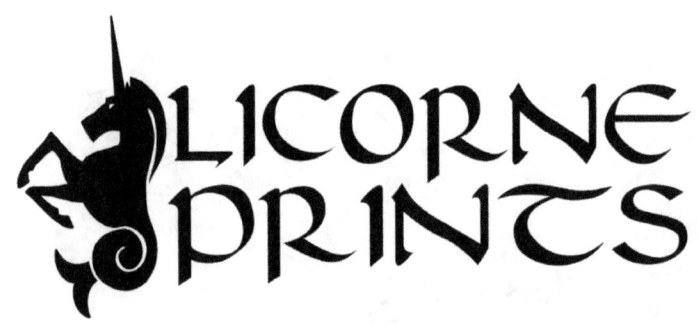

LICORNE PRINTS IS A DIVISION OF THE BMS GROUP DEDICATED TO HIGH QUALITY REPRINTS OF HISTORICAL COMIC BOOK STORIES AND NOVELS.

TO CONTACT LICORNE PRINTS DIRECTLY WRITE AT:
LICORNE@BEMYSTUDIO.COM

OR

CHECK THE LICORNE WEBSITE AT:
WWW.LICORNEPRINTS.COM

www.ingramcontent.com/pod-product-compliance
Lightning Source LLC
Chambersburg PA
CBHW081450220526
45466CB00008B/2585